CAMBRIDGE LIBRARY COLLECTION

Books of enduring scholarly value

Printing and Publishing History

The interface between authors and their readers is a fascinating subject in its own right, revealing a great deal about social attitudes, technological progress, aesthetic values, fashionable interests, political positions, economic constraints, and individual personalities. This part of the Cambridge Library Collection reissues classic studies in the area of printing and publishing history that shed light on developments in typography and book design, printing and binding, the rise and fall of publishing houses and periodicals, and the roles of authors and illustrators. It documents the ebb and flow of the book trade supplying a wide range of customers with products from almanacs to novels, bibles to erotica, and poetry to statistics.

Records of the House of Newbery

Arthur Le Blanc Newbery's family history, published in 1911, is meticulously researched and easy to read, consolidating a range of resources to provide a comprehensive history of the Newberys. Presented in timeline form using extracts from the various sources, it also includes biographies of members of the related Raikes, Le Blanc, and McClintock families. Central to the history is the life of John Newbery (1713-1767), a well-known publisher, most notably of children's books, and friend of Samuel Johnson and and Oliver Goldsmith. His relationship with the two men is well documented, and the account is supplemented with extracts from their biographies. Other notable ancestors of Le Blanc Newbery whom he includes in this book are John's son and nephew, both called Francis, the latter of whom first published Goldsmith's *The Vicar of Wakefield*; and Admiral Sir Francis Leopold McClintock (1819-1907), the Arctic explorer.

Cambridge University Press has long been a pioneer in the reissuing of out-of-print titles from its own backlist, producing digital reprints of books that are still sought after by scholars and students but could not be reprinted economically using traditional technology. The Cambridge Library Collection extends this activity to a wider range of books which are still of importance to researchers and professionals, either for the source material they contain, or as landmarks in the history of their academic discipline.

Drawing from the world-renowned collections in the Cambridge University Library, and guided by the advice of experts in each subject area, Cambridge University Press is using state-of-the-art scanning machines in its own Printing House to capture the content of each book selected for inclusion. The files are processed to give a consistently clear, crisp image, and the books finished to the high quality standard for which the Press is recognised around the world. The latest print-on-demand technology ensures that the books will remain available indefinitely, and that orders for single or multiple copies can quickly be supplied.

The Cambridge Library Collection will bring back to life books of enduring scholarly value (including out-of-copyright works originally issued by other publishers) across a wide range of disciplines in the humanities and social sciences and in science and technology.

Records of the House of Newbery

From 1274 to 1910

Arthur Le Blanc Newbery

CAMBRIDGE
UNIVERSITY PRESS

CAMBRIDGE UNIVERSITY PRESS

Cambridge, New York, Melbourne, Madrid, Cape Town, Singapore,
São Paolo, Delhi, Dubai, Tokyo

Published in the United States of America by Cambridge University Press, New York

www.cambridge.org
Information on this title: www.cambridge.org/9781108012805

© in this compilation Cambridge University Press 2010

This edition first published 1911
This digitally printed version 2010

ISBN 978-1-108-01280-5 Paperback

Records of the House of Newbery

NATUS 1713.   OBIIT 1767.

from 1274 to 1910

with 15 Likenesses and other Illustrations, etc.

PRINTED BY BEMROSE & SONS LIMITED
DERBY AND LONDON
1911

The Newberys
in Six Generations

NATUS 1713. OBIIT 1767.

Some of Their Likenesses

. . . and . . .

showing how their name was spelt in 1274, etc.

PREFACE.

TO achieve the object of this exceedingly abbreviated history in so few pages as are occupied with this appreciation, and to force into it the likenesses, dates, and various matters of interest and history concerning the Newbery, Raikes, Le Blanc, and McClintock families herein collected, has been a task involving much arrangement, time, expense, research, and patience.

Many interesting lines of thought have been sacrificed, because the intention has been to bring into prominence in it those members of each family who have made their history what it is, and whose names have been handed down in books of notable writers as worthy of remembrance, and have contributed to their maintenance, guidance, and stability.

This does not mean that those to whom no reference has been made deserve no mention; far from it. The history of the earlier families ceased, and available records no longer were kept, after the death in 1818 of Francis Newbery, leaving a gap of ninety-three years to the present time.

This humble effort to collect what was obtainable from every known source leaves much to be desired. It may rescue persons from oblivion and keep intact a nucleus upon which others, better qualified, may improve.

The compiling of these histories has been a long but very interesting labour of love, recalling memories of relatives who have passed away and mentioning others who remain. The printing of two hundred copies at 8s. 6d. each has been costly.

Mr. Arthur Le Blanc Newbery will count himself well rewarded by a kind reception being accorded to his endeavour to bring together, collate, arrange, and at the same time preserve these facts.

He owes his obligations to Boswell's "Life of Dr. Johnson," to Washington Irving's "Biography of Oliver Goldsmith," and to Welsh's history, "A Bookseller of the Last Century" (1885), for information from their works referring to his great-grandfather, John Newbery, and his publications, his great-uncle, Robert Raikes, and his Sunday Schools.

He acknowledges his indebtedness among others to "The Records of My Life," by John Taylor, 1882 (ii. 204), Prior's "Life of Goldsmith," Boehm's edition of Goldsmith's works (Ed. Gibbs), Forster's "Life of Goldsmith," "Robert Raikes, Journalist and Philanthropist" (Hodder and Stoughton), The British Museum Library, and the manuscript and autobiography in the possession of the family.

Rubbish of one generation is the treasure of the next. What is passing unheeded to-day will be the material for history to-morrow. Hence these lines.

"*Elmhurst*,"
High Barnet, Herts.,
April, 1911.

INDEX TO ILLUSTRATIONS.

FIFTEEN LIKENESSES, INCLUDING A MEMBER
OF EACH OF THE SIX GENERATIONS.

Of the Family of the Newberys from 1274. Edward I. and onwards.

FROM the Indexes to be found in the Literary Search Room, Record Office, Chancery Lane, London, the following references have been taken :—

Vol. xi., Rotuli Hundredorum Com. Buk. Edw. I., 1274. anno 1274, Burgus de Marlawe, page 354 : D'dca dua cowia tenet Henr' de Newbur unu burg redd' p. annu dce xvij d. D'dco J. tenet Henr' de Newbury unu wantam, &c., redd' eidem p. annu xvj d.

Vol. i., *temp.* Hen. III. and Edw. I., page 10, Rotuli Hundredorum Nywbyri. It wills clic balls Alic de la Marche de Nuibyr cepit cinq.

Vol. i., page 107, anno 19 Edw. I., 1274, Hen. III. to Edw. II. Calendarium, Inquis. Post Mortem Sive Escartarum, No. 83. Joh'es de Neubiry pro Hospital sancti Joh'is Jerusalem— Grenham terr', &c., Berks.

1292. Vol. i., page 165, 28 Edw. I., No. 125, anno 1292. Calendarium Inquis. Post Mortem Gervasius Newebury et alii pro Abb' e de Middelton, Catestok, &c. ; Byestedon 3, virgat' terr' et in Upsydeleng ; 4, virgat terr', Dorset.

1293.   Vol. i., page 107, 19 Edw. I., 1293. John de Newbiry, Berks.

1356.   Vol. ii., page 195, 29 Edw. III., 1356. John de Newbury, Calendarium Edwardus Stocke, propavit Joh' en de Newbury. Capellanum (chaplain) et el' Rusteshale Maner, Stocke Maner, rewan eidem Edwardo, Wiltes. Calendarium Inquis. Post Mortem,

1413. No. 33, page 22, 4 Hen. 5, 1413. Will'us Newbury, Kynwersdon Mep. terr', &c., ut de maner de Templecombe, Somerset.

From the earliest years of Queen Elizabeth's reign, the names of the Newberys appear in the parish registers at Waltham St. Lawrence, near Reading, in the county of Berkshire.

There is still extant an old black-letter volume, entitled "A briefe exposition of such chapters of ye Olde Testament as usuallie are redde in the church at common praier on the Sundays, by Thomas Cooper, Bishop of Lincolne," colophon-imprinted at London by Henrie Denham for Rafe Newbery, dwelling at Fleet Streete, a little

1537. above the Conduite, anno 1537.

As this work is not enumerated in an early seventeenth century edition of the Bodleian Catalogue, it is reckoned to be very rare.

In 1543 Catharine Howard, wife of Henry VIII., died.

The following from these parochial records was kindly extracted in 1908 by the vicar, the Hon. and

2

Rev. Grey Neville, who, after 350 years, found it rather hard to make out. It is the third entry on the first page, and reads thus:—

"1559. Mar . . . 9, Willim Newberry, fil. Willim, fuit Bapt . ur." A few lines further down :—"1560, Feb. 22. Clementia Newberry, fuit Bapt . r."

After this it seems that the name occurs on every page, sometimes two or three times.

1560. Ralph Newbery carried on business as a publisher in Fleet Street, a little above the conduit, in London; was made free of the Stationers' Company January 21st, 1560, Warden in 1583, again in 1590, Master in 1598 and 1601. He gave a stock of books, and the privilege of printing, to be sold for the benefit of Christ's Hospital and Bridewell. His name appears on many of the most important publications of his day: "The Dictionary of National Biography," in the Library of the British Museum, contains a long and interesting list of them. He seems to have retired in 1605.

1563. Thomas Newbery was the author of "a Booke in Englysshe Metre of the great Marchaunt Man, called 'Dives Pragmaticus,' very preaty for children to rede, whereby they may be better, and more readyer rede and wryte about wares and implements in this world contayned."

1594. John Newbery, the brother of the above-named Ralph, was a publisher at the sign of the "Ball," in St. Paul's Churchyard, till his death in 1603.

Nathaniel Newbery pursued the same occupation from 1616 to 1634, chiefly publishing Puritan tracts.

1608. Ralph Newbery bequeathed to the poor of Waltham, in the reign of Charles II., property, the proceeds of which, now about £50 per annum, are distributed annually to the poor of the parish.

In the reign of Charles I., Humphrey Newbery, "an utter barrester of Lincoln's Inn," was buried at
1638. Waltham St. Lawrence in 1638, his wife in 1640, their daughter in 1634.

In the churchyard are many resting-places of the Newberys, and, to judge by the several records in the church, they were persons of distinction in the parish.

Robert Newbery, a landed proprietor in the neighbourhood, had a son named John, who was
1713. born in 1713, in the reign of Queen Anne; his baptism was registered July 19th. There he passed his boyhood. Being an untiring reader, he obtained a wide knowledge of literature. In 1730 he left his birthplace for Reading, and found congenial occupation as assistant to William Carnan, who the records at Somerset House, London, inform us was the proprietor and editor of the *Reading Mercury* and *Oxford Gazette*, which first appeared on July 18th, 1723, George I. being king. He died in 1737, leaving all his property to his brother Charles, and to John Newbery, appointing them his executors. The latter soon mastered the routine of the *Gazette* and *Mercury*,

4

NATUS 1713.   OBIIT 1767.

Jn Newbery

and, paying his addresses to the widow (his age was about 24), they were in due time united in wedlock. Their children were three—Mary, John, and Francis. Mary, born in 1740, married Michael Power, a Spanish merchant, in 1766, in George III.'s reign, and left a numerous family. John followed in September, 1741, living only eleven years. Christopher Smart, the poet, celebrated his memory by the following epitaph :—

> " Henceforth be every tender fear supprest,
>   Or let us weep for joy, that he is blest ;
>   From grief to bliss, from earth to heav'n remov'd,
>   His mem'ry honoured, as his life belov'd ;
>   That heart o'er which no evil e'er had power,
>   That disposition sickness could not sour,
>   That sense, so oft to riper years denied,
>   That patience heroes might have owned with pride ;
>   His painful race undauntedly he ran,
>   And in the eleventh winter died a man."

Their father, John Newbery, whose fame as a publisher is partly founded on the books for children he produced and his connection with Oliver Goldsmith and Dr. Johnson, left no field untried in his publishing ventures. He had shares in various magazines (and employed them both to contribute occasional essays) and in the *London Chronicle, Lloyd's Evening Post, Owen's Chronicle, The Westminster Journal,* and *Yeovil Mercury.*

1740. The surviving Newberys have a list of the books published by their ancestors from 1740 to 1800, which occupies 79 pages in Welsh's History

5

of John Newbery. It comprises theology, fiction, prose, poetry, scientific and educational works, and music; and, indeed, every department of literature is represented.

In the course of a journey by coach into Lancashire, he wrote to his wife—"At almost every parish in this county there is a very useful instrument called a Ducking Stool, where the women are cured of scolding," &c. After making a tour of England, his common-place books shed some curious light upon the manners and customs of his time.

1743. On July 6th, 1743, the youngest child, Francis, was born, and, as we shall see, succeeded to the business of which his father, John Newbery, was then so busy in laying the foundations. Three or four years afterwards he transferred it to London, for the more ready disposal of a variety of publications which were printed at Reading, and of which he was either the author, compiler, or publisher.

In 1743 John Newbery entered into and signed an agreement with John Hooper, Surgeon, of Reading, with a view of aiding and developing his practice. This project proved profitable to both of them; in some respects, it is holding good 168 years after they jointly signed it. The Newberys of to-day are its custodians, and other documents of like import are in excellent preservation.

Having now opened a business house in London, 1744. on December 8th, 1744, in the 18th year of the reign of King George II., His Majesty sent "to his trusty and well-beloved " John Newbery, greeting, his royal privilege and license to publish a work entitled "The Circle of the Sciences," in seven volumes. Vol. 1.— Grammar made easy. Humbly inscribed to His Highness Prince Wm. Henry. Price bound 6d. Vol. 2.— Arithmetic made easy. Humbly inscribed to His Highness Prince Edward Augustus. Price bound 1/-. Vol. 3.—Rhetorick made easy, and illustrated by several beautiful orations from Demosthenes, Cicero, Sallust, Homer, Shakespeare, Milton, etc. Humbly inscribed to His Highness Prince George. Price bound 1/-. Vol. 4.—Poetry made easy, and embellished with a great variety of epigrams, epitaphs, songs, odes, pastorals, etc., from the best authors. Humbly inscribed to Her Highness the Princess Augusta. Price bound 1/-. Vol. 5.—Logick made easy, to which is added a compendious system of Metaphysics, or Ontology. Price bound 1/-. Vol. 6.— Geography made easy, and embellished with cuts. Humbly inscribed to the Marquis of Blandford, as the last was to the Marquis of Tavistock. Price bound 1/6. Vol. 7.—Chronology made easy, to which is added a table of the most memorable events from the beginning of the world to the year 1747. Humbly inscribed to the Earl of Dufton. Price bound 1/-. His branch establishment was in Devereux Court, Temple, and was opened in this year.

Newbery was probably one of the most ingenious advertisers of his day, and his ingenuity was in most cases rewarded with success. He was almost as great in the art of puffing his wares as the immortal Puff himself, and he employed the puff of every kind. "The *puff direct*, the *puff preliminary*, the *puff collateral*, the *puff collusive*, and the *puff oblique*, or the *puff by implication*," were all used in their turn, and no little skill was displayed in their concoction.

It may be interesting to give some specimens of how he applied his knowledge. The following are some of his methods of announcing his little books and keeping them before the world. From the "Penny *Morning Post*" of June 18th, 1744, we cull the following :—

1744.

"According to Act of Parliament (neatly bound and gilt) a pretty little pocket book, intended for the instruction and amusement of little Master Tommy and pretty Miss Molly, with an agreeable letter to each from Jack the Giant Killer; as, also, a Ball and Pincushion, the use of which will infallibly make Tommy a good boy and Polly a good girl. To the whole is prefixed a letter on education, humbly addressed to all parents, guardians, governesses, etc., wherein rules are laid down for making their children strong, healthy, wise, and happy. Printed for J. Newbery, at the Bible and Crown, near Devereux Court, without Temple Bar. Price of the book, 6d.; with a Ball and Pincushion, 8d."

8

1751.   Seven years later (March 1st, 1751) the following appeared in the public prints :—

"To all little good boys and girls."

"MY DEAR FRIENDS,—You are desired not to be uneasy that the publication of your 'Lilliputian Magazine' is deferred till Saturday. The whole is printed, and all the servants of the Society are employed in making them up for you; but as the number is so large, 'twill be impossible to get them perfected before that time. I am, my dear friends, yours affectionately, R. Goodwill, Secretary. From my office at the Bible and Sun, in St. Paul's Church-yard, February 28th, 1751."

"It has been said, and said wisely, that the only way to remedy the depravity of human nature and the corrupt principles of mankind is to begin with the rising generation and to take the mind in its infant state and susceptible of any impression; to represent their duties and future interests in a manner that shall seem rather intended to amuse than instruct; to warm their affections with such subjects as are capable of giving them delight and of impressing on their tender minds proper sentiments of religion, justice, honour, and virtue."

> "When infant reason grows apace, it calls
> For the kind hand of an assiduous care;
> Delightful task! To rear the tender thought,
> To teach the young idea how to shoot,
> To pour instruction o'er the mind,
> To breathe th' inspiring spirit, to implant
> The generous purpose in the glowing breast."
>   THOMSON.

9

"How far Mr. Newbery's little books may tend to forward this good work may be in some measure seen by what are already published, and, it is presumed, will more evidently appear by others which are now in the press."

1745.   In consequence of Dr. James, of Bruton Street, London—the author of a medical dictionary, in three immense volumes, to which his schoolfellow Dr. Samuel Johnson wrote the preface—agreeing that John Newbery should take a half-share in the profits accruing from the sale of his fever powder in consideration of his introducing it, did Fate see fit to turn the course of John Newbery's life into a new channel.

These three volumes were published in 1745, are in fine condition, and can be seen in Charterhouse Square.

With the signing of this partnership deed, still preserved, in the 20th year of George II., May 25th, 1745, was laid the foundation of a branch of business which has called for, employed the energies, and rewarded the labours of five generations of Newberys, of which the present consists of four members, bearing the old name—two of them, thank God, having stood the wear of half a century. They acted as pioneers, now do so as guides, training their sons to take their places.

A stoppered bottle of Dr. James' Powder, prepared by Dr. James himself, who died in 1776, aged 75, has been preserved. A packet similarly prepared is kept in their museum for analysis, if need be, by the Pharmaceutical Society of Great Britain. It is also interesting that the oldest impression in the proof book kept in the stamping department at Somerset House, London, is an appropriated stamp for Dr. James' Fever Powder, F. Newbery & Sons.

1746. In 1746, the 20th year of George II., a Scottish Lord was beheaded.

1747. In 1747 Lord Lovat was the last executed on Tower Hill.

1748. In No. 378 of the *Whitehall Evening Post, or London Intelligencer*, of Tuesday, July 12th, to Thursday, July 14th, 1748, is exhibited an illustration of the Banqueting Hall and the mounted Horse Guards opposite in Whitehall Place on the front page, and on the last is an announcement that His Majesty, having been most graciously pleased to grant to Robert James, Doctor in Physic, his royal letters patent for the sole use of the powder, and the said Dr. James in virtue thereof appointed John Newbery the only vendor and disposer of it, as appears in an advertisement in the *London Gazette* of the 12th instant.

On this date, and in the same number, is the following :—" General Post Office, July 12th, 1748. Public Notice is hereby given that the correspondence by letter, between these kingdoms and the kingdom of France is now opened, and that the first mail, for the said kingdom of France, will be forwarded from this office on Monday next, the 18th of this instant July."

In *The Whitehall Evening Post, or London Intelligencer,* Tuesday to Thursday, May 3rd, 1753, No. 1127, Price 1½d., we read that "the King has "caused an ordinance to be published renewing the "former prohibition against sending gold, either in "bars or specie, out of the Kingdom, and for inflict-"ing severe punishment on those who shall for the "future be found guilty of it."

"Tuesday, the sacred oratorio, called 'Messiah,' was "performed in the chapel of the Foundling Hospital, "under the direction of the inimitable composer "thereof, George Frederick Handel, Esq., who, in the "organ concerto, played himself a Voluntary on the "fine organ he gave to that chapel. His new Te "Deum, Jubilate, and Coronation anthem, with an "anthem by Dr. Boyce, will be vocally and "instrumentally performed on Tuesday, May 8th, "1753."

A spelling Dictionary of the English language on a new plan, so contrived as to take up no more room in the pocket than a common snuff box, was published by Jno. Newbery, by the King's authority, at the "Bible and Sun," in St. Paul's Churchyard. This number also contains an announcement concerning Dr. James' Powder, bearing John Newbery's name and address as above.

Robert Newbery's letter to his brother John, at the "Bible and Sun," in St. Paul's Churchyard, London, is an interesting relic, well preserved, from Waltham St. Lawrence, dated January 19th, 1753.

One-twelfth share of "The Gentleman's Magazine" was purchased by Newbery in 1755, for £333 6s. 8d.

1755. A writer in *The World*, No. 115, March 13th, 1755, in a somewhat satirical paper jocularly proposed to dispose of the volumes of *The World* at 3/- per volume, declaring that to relieve the unhappy is the full end of this publication. A friend called and showed him Jno. Newbery's announcement—"This day was published 'Nurse Truelove's New Year's Gift,' or, the book of books for children, adorned with cuts and designed as a present for every little boy who would become a great man and ride upon a fine horse, and to every little girl who would become a great woman and ride in a Lord Mayor's coach. Printed for the author, who has ordered these books to be *given gratis* to all little boys and girls at the Bible and Sun, in St. Paul's Churchyard. They paying for the binding, which is only twopence each book." This completely altered the passing off of the volumes of *The World*, for they were advertised as *gratis at every bookseller's shop* in town to all sorts of persons, they only paying 9/- *for the binding*.

Another means Newbery employed to make his books known was by bringing in allusions to them in the text of the stories. Everyone who has read "Goody Two Shoes" will recall the incident of little Margery's father's death. He was "seized with a violent fever in a place where Dr. James' Fever Powder was not to be had, and where he died miserably." In the same book we find, "She then sung the Cuzz's chorus (which may be found in the 'Little Pretty Plaything,' published by Mr. Newbery)." In another little book, "Fables in Verse," the following occurs:—"Woglog at Bath. Lady,— 'Well, Mr. Woglog, where have you been?' 'At church, Madam.' 'And pray, my lady, where have you been?' 'Drinking the waters,' said she. 'But not for *health?*' 'No, truly; I only drink them for *wantonness.*' 'Well, Madam, and they cured you of *that complaint?*' says Mr. Woglog. The lady blushed, and took a turn on the Grand Parade, while Woglog stepped into Mr. Leake's to read one of Mr. Newbery's little books."

Dr. Johnson made John Newbery the subject of one of his essays in the "Idler" No. 19, Saturday, 1758. August 19th, 1758, rather a caricature than a portrait, but the likeness in some of the features was just and appropriate. The publication was taken in good part by Newbery, who, however, threatened to return the compliment by depicting the Doctor, with his peculiarities, in a subsequent number.

Dr. Johnson styled John Newbery "the great

14

"philosopher, whose business keeps him in perpetual
"motion, and whose motion always eludes his
"business, who is always to do what he never does,
"who cannot stand still, because he is wanted in
"another place, and who is wanted in many places
"because he stays in none."

Malcolm, in his "Londinium Redivivum," says :
"Newbery for many years issued shoals of little
"useful publications for children, a library which I
"well remember possessing when nearly 4,000 miles
"from England, and I date my first partiality for
"literature to have arisen from the *splendid bindings*
"and *beautiful engravings* of Newbery."

At the "Bible and Sun," in St. Paul's Churchyard, John Newbery combined with his work of a
publisher the business of medicine merchant on a
large scale. His announcements in the newspapers
of that day are evidence of the joint concerns. He
especially identified himself with several newspaper
enterprises in London and the provinces, employ-
ing eminent authors to write for his periodicals,
and projected *The Universal Chronicle or Weekly
Gazette,* in which Johnson's papers called "The
Idler" were first printed. In *The Public Ledger*
Goldsmith's "Citizen of the World" first saw the
light. Newbery undertook the separate publication
of "The Idler" and "The Rambler," as well as
Johnson's "Lives of the Poets," and thus came into
close connection with Dr. Johnson.

Oliver Goldsmith seems to have written for his "Literary Magazine" as early as 1757. In 1762 he went to reside in a country lodging at Islington, kept by a relative of the publisher, and, when the poet was in dire straits, Newbery advanced him £11 upon "The Traveller." Another of Newbery's literary clients, Christopher Smart, married his step-daughter, Anna Maria Carnan. The unfortunate Dr. William Dodd, who was hanged for forgery, was connected, like Smollett, with the "British Magazine." He also edited from 1760 to 1767 the first religious magazine, which was projected by Newbery in 1760, and was styled "The Christian Magazine."

The oft quoted paragraph from "The Vicar of Wakefield," which perhaps has helped as much as anything to keep Newbery's name alive, and his memory fresh to all generations, must be cited in this connection. "'It is possible,' said good Dr. "Primrose, 'the anxiety from the last circumstance "'alone might have brought on a relapse, had I not "'been supplied by a traveller who stopped to take "'a cursory sort of refreshment. This person was "'no other than the philanthropic bookseller in St. "'Paul's Churchyard, who has written so many books "'for children. He called himself their friend, but "'he was the friend of all mankind.'" It was ever a favourite topic with Oliver Goldsmith to tell pleasant stories of Newbery, who, he said, was the patron of more distressed authors than any man of his time, and that Goldsmith had a high opinion of him is made further evident from the following charade which he wrote :—

> " What we say of a thing which is just come in fashion,
> And that which we do with the dead,
> Is the name of the honestest man in creation ;
> What more of a man can be said ? "

He wrote for the literary magazines set on foot by John Newbery.

The agreement, dated March 25th, 1758, signed by the eleven shareholders who owned the sixteen shares in the *Lloyd's Evening Post* and *British Chronicle*, is interesting reading. The largest part proprietor was John Newbery, who possessed three shares. His great grandsons in Charterhouse Square have preserved No. 319 of volume 5, for August 1st - 3rd, 1759, which shows the one halfpenny government stamp, 150 years old. It contains on page 114, " A Comic Poem on a Serious Subject," comprised in 140 lines. Here follow six of them :—

> " That is a writer, Sir, of note,
> From sundry books expect to quote,
> Learn'd and sagacious to transcribe,
> New work from all the ancient tribe
> Of authors, who have wrote before,
> Who dy'd, perhaps, extremely poor."

John Newbery, in 1758, intending to prepare his son Francis for the medical profession, by the advice of Dr. James entered him in the fifth form of Merchant Taylors' school in London, under Mr. Criche, the headmaster, and he ingratiated himself into the master's good opinion, who honoured him so far as to desire him to carry his wig to his barber's in Cannon Street. Though not much delighted with the errand, yet, as the boys were playing in the cloisters under the school, he, thinking to turn this indignity to account, put the huge periwig on his own head, and opening the door, let the toupee only appear. The boys were instantly on the scamper, and he in the great busby ran after them roaring out, "Pshaw, ye rogues, I'll bang ye to pieces." The Rev. James Townley succeeded Mr. Criche as headmaster, and David Garrick, an intimate friend of his, accommodated him with a set of scenes that his pupils might perform "The Eunuch of Terence." To Frank Newbery was assigned the character of Gnatho. Garrick was pleased and complimented him in consequence with the handsome offer of a free admission to Drury Lane Theatre.

Boswell's "Life of Johnson," page 227. An enquiry into the state of foreign countries was an object that seemed at all times to have interested Dr. Johnson, hence John Newbery found no great difficulty in persuading him to write the introduction to a collection of voyages and travels published by him under the title of "The World

Displayed," the first volume of which appeared in 1759, and was advertised in the *London Chronicle* in that year.

Besides the loose copies of ancient newspapers, one bound volume of the *London Chronicle*, Jan. 30th to Feb. 1st, 1759, page 105, contains a letter in French, occupying a page and a half, with translation, from the Queen of Scots to Queen Elizabeth.

In the No. 5 bound volume of the *London Chronicle* and *Evening Post* for 1759, among the Newbery advertisements, and leading articles, are numbers of "The Idler," by Dr. Johnson, No. 78 being on page 572, December 13th-15th. On page 158 of bound volume 62, 1787, is Robert Burns's "Ode to Despondency."

> "Oppress'd with grief, oppressed with care,
> A burthen more than I can bear,
> I set me down and sigh :
> Oh, life ! thou art a galling load,
> Along a rough, a weary road,
> To wretches such as I.
> Dim backward as I cast my view,
> What sickening scenes appear !
> What sorrows yet may pierce me thro',
> Too justly I may fear !
> Still caring, despairing
> Must be my bitter doom :
> My woes here shall close ne'er,
> But with the closing tomb."

Here follow five more stanzas. Also on the same

page, "An Epitaph to a Limb of the Law, on whom someone had fastened his paw."

The first number of "The Public Ledger," on January 12th, 1759, was a bold effort of John Newbery's, and the inventive head which planned "The Universal Chronicle," with the good taste that enlisted Dr. Johnson in its service, secured to the business men of those days a daily register of commerce and intelligence, which the Mark Lane merchants and shippers of to-day find useful. Goldsmith became entitled to receive two guineas from John Newbery for his first week's contribution to its pages. The No. 22,393 new series of "The Public Ledger" was published on Monday, July 6th, 1908, showing a healthy life and a successful usefulness during 150 years.

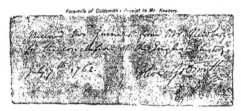

Facsimile of Goldsmith's Receipt to Mr Newbery.

FACSIMILE OF GOLDSMITH'S RECEIPT TO MR. NEWBERY.
(Reproduced by permission of Messrs. Cassell & Co., Ltd.)

In the *London Chronicle* for December 19th, 1759, John Newbery inserted the following :—" The "philosophers, politicians, necromancers, and the "learned in every faculty are desired to observe "that on the 1st of January, being New Year's

"day (oh, that we all may lead new lives!), Mr.
"Newbery intends to publish the following important
"volumes and hereby invites all his little friends,
"who are good, to call for them at the Bible
"and Sun, in St. Paul's Churchyard, but those
"who are naughty to have none."

The bound volume of the *London Chronicle*, 1787,
see heading June 30th, giving No. 4783, to page
624; July 3-5 contains five poetical pieces;
on page 619, date December 27-29, is given a list of
thirteen of Newbery's new publications for the instruction and entertainment of young ladies and gentlemen
in the Christmas holidays. No. 1 is the looking-
glass for the mind, an intellectual mirror, being
an elegant collection of the most delightful little
stories and interesting tales, price 2s. 6d., bound;
also may be had every other useful book for young
people, together with dissected maps of different
countries, geographical pastimes, and various sorts
of cards. The names, particulars, and cost of
twelve other books follow. The name of Francis
Newbery is substituted for John Newbery's after the
latter's death, and his name to advertisements appears
four times on pages 78 and 79 in the 1787 volume.

The *London Chronicle* bound volume contains
several announcements of the "Philosophia Brit-
annica," 2nd edition, 3 vols., price 18s., bound,
printed for John Newbery, in St. Paul's Churchyard,
609 pages. No. 89 of "The Idler" faces it on

page 504. "This day is published by John Newbery, at the Bible and Sun, in St. Paul's Churchyard, together with poetry, prologues, nearly a column of verses on Christmas Day," etc.

1761. Memorandum of agreement was entered into 19th September, 1761 (when Lord Bute was Prime Minister on the accession of George III.), between John Newbery, of St. Paul's Churchyard, and Robert Raikes, of Gloucester, to carry out mutual transactions profitable to both.

1762. In June, 1762, John Newbery accompanied his son Francis to Oxford, where he entered at Trinity College. Mr. Warton, who was his tutor there, with others, established the Jelly Bag Society, of which a linen cap, striped, and terminating in a point, was the token at their meetings. This originated the following epigram by John Newbery :—

> " One day, in Christchurch meadows walking,
> Of poetry and such things talking,
>   Says Ralph—a merry wag—
> ' An epigram, if smart and good,
> In all its circumstances should
>   Be like a jelly bag.'
> ' Your simile, I own, is new,
> But, how wilt make it out?' says Hugh.
>   Quoth Ralph, ' I'll tell thee, friend,
> Make it at top, both large and fit
> To hold a budget full of wit,
>   And point it at the end !
> If true, that notion, which but few contest,
> That, in the way of wit, short things are best.
> Then, in good epigrams two virtues meet,
> For, 'tis their glory to be short and sweet.' "

FROM THE PORTRAIT BY ROMNEY

SI RECTE PERSTES

Fra.ˢ Newbery

FRANCIS NEWBERY, born 1743, died 1818.

As a short course of lectures in anatomy was given annually at Cambridge, Francis Newbery, who had become tolerably proficient in London, offered his services gratuitously to Dr. Collignon, M.D., Professor of Anatomy, in dissecting and preparing the bodies for the lectures.

Dr. Johnson aided the launching of "The Traveller" by a favourable notice in the "Critical Review." But one of the highest testimonials was given by Miss Reynolds, sister of Sir Joshua. Dr. Johnson read it aloud from beginning to end in her presence. "Well," exclaimed she, "I never more shall think Dr. Goldsmith ugly." Its appearance at once altered Goldsmith's standing— Boswell was astonished to find him whom he had so much undervalued suddenly elevated to a par with his idol. "He imitates you, sir," said he to Dr. Johnson. "Why no, sir," replied Johnson, "Jack Hawkesworth is one of my imitators, but not Goldsmith. Goldy, sir, has great merit." "But, sir, he is much indebted to you for getting so high in the public estimation." "Why, sir, he has, perhaps, got *sooner* to it by his intimacy with me." Washington Irving says, "It produced a golden harvest to Mr. "Newbery," of whom he added, "he was a worthy, "intelligent, kind-hearted man, and a reasonable, "though cautious friend to authors, relieving them with "loans, taking care to be well repaid by the labour "of their pens." Good fortune is of comparatively little use without hard work, and John Newbery never spared himself. He is another example of what untiring energy, indomitable perseverance, and enthusiastic love of work can do. He sought the right groove for his talents with unremitting zeal, and when he had found it, he applied himself vigorously to work in it.

History has it that he was ingenious in his mode of advertising. He had well learned the lesson Dryden teaches in the following lines :—

> "New books, we know, require a puff,
> A title to entrap the eyes,
> And catch the reader by surprise.
> Children, like tender oziers, take the bow,
> And, as they first are fashioned, always grow."

Or, as Pope puts it,

> " Just as the twig is bent, the tree's inclined ;
> 'Tis education forms the vulgar mind."

Though so exclusively a picture of British scenes and manners, "The Vicar of Wakefield" has been translated into almost every language, and everywhere its charm has been the same. Goethe, the great genius, declared in his 81st year that it was his delight at the age of twenty, and that he read it again from beginning to end with renewed delight.

Washington Irving, in his biography of Oliver Goldsmith, has it that new advances were

TEMPLE BAR.

"JOHNSON.—I remember once being with Goldsmith in Westminster Abbey.
While we surveyed the Poets' Corner, I said to him
  '*Forsitan et nostrum nomen miscebitur istis.*'
When we got to Temple Bar, he stopped me, pointed to the heads
  upon it, and slily whispered me
    '*Forsitan et nostrum nomen miscebitur* ISTIS.

(BOSWELL'S " LIFE OF JOHNSON.")

procured from Newbery by Goldsmith on the promise of a new tale in the style of the "Vicar of Wakefield," of which he showed him a few roughly sketched chapters. Garrick was present, and played the part of master of the revels, for he was an intimate friend of the master of the house. Out at Merry Islington, in Canonbury House, Dr. Samuel Johnson, Oliver Goldsmith, and John Newbery had chambers, and resided there in quiet seclusion. This had been a hunting lodge of Queen Elizabeth, in whose time it was surrounded by park and forest. John Newbery was Goldsmith's banker, and kept up a kind of running account, sometimes for pounds, sometimes for shillings. Among others, it is suggested, and with great probability, that he wrote for John Newbery the famous nursery story

1765. of "Goody Two-Shoes," which appeared in 1765, at a moment when Goldsmith was writing, and much pressed for funds. The following lines, with the means by which she acquired learning and wisdom, and in consequence thereof her estate, were set forth for the benefit of those :—

> " Who, from a state of rags and care,
> And having shoes but half a pair,
> Their fortune and their fame should fix,
> And gallop in a coach and six."

Washington Irving, in his "LIFE OF GOLDSMITH," wrote: "Several quaint little tales introduced in his essays show that he had a turn for this species of MOCK history: and the advertisements and title-pages bear the stamp of his sly and playful humour."

John Newbery had the honour of pecuniarily assisting Dr. Samuel Johnson and Dr. Oliver Goldsmith, and publishing their works. In Washington Irving's life of Oliver Goldsmith, his name occurs twenty-three times in connection with many others living in those days.

In the Library of the British Museum has been preserved a small volume, 4½ ins. by 3 ins., entitled "Fables in Verse for the Improvement of the Young and Old, by Abraham Æsop, Esq., to which are added fables in verse and prose, with the conversation of birds and beasts at their several meetings, routs, and assemblies: by Woglog, the great giant, 140 pages. Illustrated with a variety of curious cuts by the best masters, and with an account of the lives of the authors by their old friend Mr. Newbery—

"'The truth, I hope, you won't dispute,
When told you by a brother brute.'"

Letter from Leo, the Great Lion; the 5th edition, London.

"Printed for the booksellers of all nations, and sold at the Bible and Sun, in St. Paul's Churchyard, 1765 (price 6d., bound)." At the end the last pages are devoted to a list as follows:—

1. The Little Lottery Book.
2. The Little Pretty Pocket-book.
3. The Infant Tutor.
4. Be Merry and Wise.
5. A Collection of Pretty Poems.
6. A Pretty Book for Children.
7. A Pretty Book of Pictures for Little Masters and Misses.
8. The Lilliputian Magazine.
9. The Museum for Young Gentlemen and Ladies.
10. A Collection of Pretty Poems.
11. The Philosophy of Tops and Balls.
12. Letters on the More Common Occasions in Life.
13. The Holy Bible Abridged.
14. A Pocket Dictionary.
15. An Easy Spelling Dictionary.

It takes only a slight effort of imagination to see John Newbery and his two friends, Dr. Johnson

JOHN NEWBERY RECEIVING OLIVER GOLDSMITH
ON THE INTRODUCTION OF DR. JOHNSON.

and Oliver Goldsmith, discussing books and medicine in his house situated on the north-west corner of St. Paul's.

Dr. Johnson, who was a Lichfield man and a friend of Dr. James's, introduced John Newbery to him.

27

About this time, Goldsmith was engaged by Dr. Smollett, who was about to launch "The British Magazine." Smollett was a complete schemer and speculator in literature, and intent upon enterprises that had money, rather than reputation, in view. Goldsmith had a good-humoured wit at this propensity in one of his papers in "The Bee," in which he represents Johnson, Hume, and others, taking seats in the stage coach bound for Fame, while Smollett prefers that destined for Riches.

"'I received one morning,' says Dr. Johnson, 'a "'message from poor Goldsmith that he was in great "'distress, and as it was not in his power to come to "'me, begging I would go to him as soon as possible. "'He told me he had a manuscript ready for the "'press, which he produced to me. I looked into "'it, and saw its merit, and told the landlady I "'would soon return, and having gone to Newbery's, "'sold it to him for sixty pounds.'" This was "The Vicar of Wakefield," in which Goldsmith introduced John Newbery in a humorous, yet friendly manner. Recently, a 1766 "Vicar of Wakefield" sold for £88 at a book sale.

1766. Goldsmith sought a rural retreat in the summer with strolls about the then green fields of Merrie Islington, where, at Canonbury House, he and John Newbery lived. The following is a description of the spot in those days:—

"See, on the distant Slope, Majestic shows
Old Canonbury's tow'r, an ancient pile
To various fates assigned, and where, by turns,
Meanness and grandeur have alternate reigned.
Thither, in latter days, hath genius fled
From yonder city, to respire, and die.
There the sweet bard of Auburn sat, and turn'd
The plaintive moanings of his village dirge;
There learned Chambers treasured lore for men
And Newbery there his A B C's for babes."

Fox.

The literature provided for children before John
Newbery began to make it his business to cater
specially for them was of the very scantiest character.
Mr. John Ashton, in his interesting book, "Social
Life in the Reign of Queen Anne," however, tells us
that even in the early days of the last century the
little folk had their special literature. For, he says,
"there was compiled and printed a play-book for
children, to allure them to read as soon as they
can speak plain; composed of small pages, so as
not to tire children; printed with a fair and pleasing
letter, the matter and method plainer and easier
than any yet extant. The price of this was fourpence; and it must have been a favourite, for it is
advertised as being in its second edition in 1703.
Certainly the little ones then lacked many advantages
in this way that ours now possess; but, on the other
hand, so much was not required of them. There
was no dreaded 'examination' to prepare for—no
doing lessons all day long, and then working hard

at night to get ready for the next day's toil. They were not taught half a dozen languages, and all the 'ologies, whilst still in the nursery; but were the suggestions and advice given to 'the Mother' in Steele's 'Lady's Library' thoroughly carried out, they would grow up good men and women! The boys, however, had strong meat provided for them in such tales as 'Jack and the Giants,' etc."

Jno. Newbery was the first to make the issue of books specially intended for children an important branch of a publishing business; he manifested those gifts as a student, so conspicuous in after life, which education can but foster yet cannot create. The tiny volumes in his "Juvenile Library" were bound in flowered and gilt Dutch paper, the secret of the manufacture of which has been lost. They included "The Renowned History of Giles Gingerbread, a Little Boy who lived upon Learning," "Tommy Trip and his Dog Towler," and many more of a like interesting character. He also inaugurated "The Lilliputian Magazine," 1722-1786. The authorship of these "classics of the nursery" is an old battle-ground. Newbery wrote and planned some of them. "He was," says Dr. Primrose in "The Vicar of Wakefield" "when we met him, actually compiling materials for the history of one Mr. Thomas Trip"; "and if this can hardly be accepted as proof positive," says Mr. Austin Dobson, "it may be asserted that to Newbery's business instinct are due those ingenious references to his different wares and publications which crop up so unexpectedly in the course of the narrative."

Newbery's portrait is for ever enshrined in the pages of "The Vicar of Wakefield"—"that glorious pillar of unshaken orthodoxy." An article in "The Idler," gently satirising Newbery as "Jack Whirler," by Dr. Johnson, confirms this. "When he enters a house, his first declaration is that he cannot sit down, and so short are his visits that he seldom appears to have come for any other reason but to say he must go." This philanthropic bookseller of St. Paul's Churchyard was plainly a bustling, multifarious, and not unkindly personage, though it is equally plain that his philanthropy was always under the watchful care of his prudence. Essentially commercial and enterprising, he exacted his money's worth of work, and kept records of his cash advances to the authors by whom he was surrounded. Jno. Newbery died December 22nd, 1767, at his house in St. Paul's Churchyard.

"Newbery was the first publisher who introduced the regular system of 'A Juvenile Library,' and gave children books in a more permanent form than the popular CHAP-BOOKS of the period. The whole of the country was systematically travelled by a class of hawkers who, besides carrying small articles for domestic and personal use and adornment, traded in ballads, almanacks, and similar literary wares.

These wandering tradesmen were called chapmen, and the little books they carried are known as chap-books. The books issued by Newbery were more durable than these chap-books, which were simply folded, and not stitched, for they were 'strongly bound and gilt.'"

"It was from unsuitable books on subjects we do not usually teach our children that John Newbery arose to deliver the children of his day, and in reading the titles of some of his earlier books it is at once seen that a new note has been struck, and a new field opened for culture and development." "There is nothing more remarkable in Mr. Newbery's little books than the originality of their style; there have been attempts to approach its simplicity—its homeliness. Great authors have tried their hands at imitating its clever adaptation to the childish intellect, but they have failed!"

"The didactic and tiresome style of the writers of the age of prose and reason is naturally reflected in many of Newbery's books, and there is little doubt that many of the clever and distinguished men whom Newbery had drawn around him had a hand in their compilation."

"Many are said to have been written by Newbery, and there is every reason to believe that the same hand which drew up the ingenious advertisements and quaint title-pages of some of them is responsible for the contents of the little book."

Mr. Forster, in his "Life of Goldsmith," says: "I believe that to Newbery the great merit is due of having first sought to reform in some material points the moral of these books." He did not thrust all naughty boys into the jaws of the dragon, nor elevate all good boys to ride in King Peppin's coach. Goldsmith said, more than once, "that he had a hankering to write for children, and if he had realized his intention of composing the fables in which little fishes and other creatures should talk, OUR children's libraries would have had one rich possession the more."

"I am strongly inclined to believe" (says Welsh) "that Goldsmith really did gratify this hankering, and had much more to do with Newbery's books for children than has been credited to him."

Dr. Johnson has written of Gilbert Walmesley, Registrar of the Ecclesiastical Court of Lichfield: "At this man's table I enjoyed many cheerful and instructive hours, with companions such as are not often found—with one who has *lengthened* and one who has *gladdened* life; with Dr. James, whose skill in physic will be long remembered; and with David Garrick, whom I hoped to have gratified with the character of our common friend."

Leigh Hunt, in his book "The Town," says "that the most illustrious of all booksellers in our boyish days, not for his great names, not for his dinners, not for his riches, that we know of, nor for any other full - grown celebrity, but for certain little penny books, radiant with gold, and rich with bad pictures, was Mr. Newbery, the famous CHILDREN'S bookseller, at the corner of St. Paul's Churchyard, next Ludgate Street."

Of these books many writers have spoken in loving recollection. John Newbery's son Francis, in somewhat high-flown phrase, wrote : "And now, ye great men of this great empire, do you not acknowledge that you owe some of that greatness to the little books addressed to you by him who was wont to style himself your old friend in St. Paul's Churchyard, and who was so good as to communicate to you wisdom, and wit, and knowledge, in books under gold covers, only paying a penny for the binding ! Ye peers and prelates, princes, we may add too, for even King George III., who had read more than any, even of his ministers, may perhaps owe his obligations to 'Goody Two Shoes,' 'The Philosophy of Tops and Balls,' and 'The renowned history of Giles Gingerbread.' So must ye also, ye chancellors, judges, counsellors, knights, squires, and gentlemen all, who were born about the middle of last century" (1750).

"*The Microcosm* was a weekly periodical conducted by Eton boys from November 6th, 1786, to July 30th, 1787, and consisted of papers in imitation of '*The Spectator.*' In the number for June 11th, 1787. Canning speaks of the instructive histories of

Mr. Thomas Thumb, Mr. John Hickathrift, and other celebrated worthies, "a true and faithful account of whose adventures and achievements may be had by the curious, and public in general, price twopence, gilt, at Mr. Newbery's, St. Paul's Churchyard."

Mr. Samuel Philips in his " Essay on Robert Southey," tells us that "as soon as the child (Southey) could read, his aunts' friends furnished him with literature from Newbery's, 'delectable histories in sixpenny books for children, splendidly bound in the flowered and gilt Dutch paper of former days,' twenty volumes, and so laid the foundation of a love of books which grew with the child's growth, and did not cease in age, even when the vacant mind and eye could only gaze in piteous though blissful imbecility upon the things they loved."

"Far higher are my ideas of the comparative excellence of Mr. Newbery's little books, and more especially of the two to which I have before alluded. In the HEROES of these a candid and impartial critic will readily agree with me that we find a very strong resemblance to those who are immortalised in Homeric song, that in Hickathrift we see pourtrayed the spirit, the prowess, and every great quality of Achilles, and in Thumb the prudence, the caution, the patience, the perseverance of Ulysses. There is, however, one peculiar advantage which the histories of the modern worthies enjoy over their ancient originals, which is, that of writing the *great* and *sublime* of epic grandeur with the *little* and the *low* of common life, and of tempering the fiercer and more glaring colours of the *marvellous* and the *terrible* with the softer shades of the *domestic* and the *familiar*. Where, in either of the great originals, shall we find so pleasing an assemblage of tender ideas, so interesting a picture of domestic employments, as the following sketch of the night preceding that in which Tom Thumb and his brethren were to be purposely lost in the wood ? "

"Now it was nine o'clock, and all the children, after eating a piece of bread and butter, were put to bed, but little Tom did not eat his, but put it in his pocket. And now all the children were fast asleep in their beds, but little Tom could not sleep for thinking of what he had heard the night before, so he got up and put on his shoes and stockings," etc. How forcibly does this passage bring to the mind of every classical reader the picture which Homer draws of Agamemnon in the tenth book of the ILIAD—

'Αλλ' οὐκ 'Ατρείδην 'Αγαμέμνονα ποιμένα λαῶν·
"Ὕπνος ἔχε γλυκερὸς, πολλὰ φρεσὶν ὁρμαίνοντα·
— - "The chiefs before their vessels lay,
And left in sleep the labours of the day ;
All but the King; with various thoughts opprest,
His country's cares lay rolling on his breast.
He rose,
\nd on his feet the shining sandals bound."

"Many of these famous little books have doubtless absolutely disappeared. Books for children, above all others, are short-lived, and vanish more success-fully than any other kind of literature. When they have served their turn and little hands have thumbed and worn them well to pieces, few people think of saving the tattered scraps. Some, however, have fortunately been preserved; but as that genial and kindly book-lover, the Rev. Richard Hooper, says : 'Books from 1730 to 1750 are more uncommon than at almost any period. Both our great University libraries are very deficient in that period, and it was only lately that the British Museum has supplied the deficiency.' "

The appearance of "The Traveller" at once altered Goldsmith's intellectual standing in the esti-mation of society; but its effect upon the club, if we may judge from the account given by Hawkins, was most ludicrous. They were lost in astonishment that a "newspaper essayist" and "bookseller's drudge" should have written such a poem.

As a testimony of cherished and well-merited affection, he dedicated "The Traveller" to his brother Henry. There is an amusing affectation of indifference as to its fate expressed in the dedication. "What re-ception a poem may find," says he, "which has neither abuse, party, nor blank verse to support it, I cannot tell, nor am I solicitous to know." The truth is, no one was more emulous and anxious for poetic fame; and never was he more anxious than in the present instance, for it was his grand stake.

Dr. Johnson aided the launching of the poem by a favourable notice in the "*Critical Review*"; other periodical works came out in its favour. Some of the author's friends complained that it did not command instant and wide popularity; that it was a poem to win, not to strike. It went on rapidly increasing in favour; in three months a second edition was issued; shortly afterwards, a third; then a fourth; and, before the year was out, the author was pronounced the best poet of his time.

On another occasion, when the merits of "The Traveller" were discussed at Reynolds's board, Langton declared "there was not a bad line in the poem, not one of Dryden's careless verses." "I was glad," observed Reynolds, "to hear Charles Fox say it was one of the finest poems in the English language." "Why was you glad?" rejoined Langton. "You surely had no doubt of this before." "No," interposed Johnson, decisively; "the merit of 'The Traveller' is so well established, that Mr. Fox's praise cannot augment it, nor his censure diminish it."

Goldsmith walked to the gardens of the "White Conduit House," so famous among the essayists of the last century. While strolling one day in these gardens, he met three females of the family of a respectable tradesman, to whom he was under some obligation. With his prompt disposition to oblige, he conducted them about the garden, treated them to tea and ran up a bill in the most open-handed manner imaginable; it was only when he came to pay that he found himself in one of his old dilemmas —he had not the wherewithal in his pocket. A scene of perplexity now took place between him and the waiter, in the midst of which came up some of his acquaintances, in whose eyes he wished to stand particularly well. This completed his mortification. There was no concealing the awkwardness of his position. The sneers of the waiter revealed it. His acquaintances amused themselves for some time at his expense, professing their inability to relieve him. When, however, they had enjoyed their banter, the waiter was paid, and poor Goldsmith enabled to convoy off the ladies with flying colours.

We hear much about "poetic inspiration," and the "poet's eye in a fine frenzy rolling"; but Sir Joshua Reynolds gives an anecdote of Goldsmith, while engaged upon his poem, calculated to cure our notions about the ardour of composition. Calling upon the poet one day, he opened the door without ceremony, and found him in the double occupation of turning a couplet and teaching a pet dog to sit upon his haunches. At one time he would glance his eye at his desk, and at another shake his finger at the dog to make him retain his position. The last lines on the page were still wet; they form a part of the description of Italy:

" By sports like these are all their cares beguiled,
The sports of children satisfy the child."

Goldsmith, with his usual good-humour, joined in the laugh caused by his whimsical employment, and acknowledged that his boyish sport with the dog suggested the stanza.

1764. The poem was published on December 19th, 1764, in a quarto form, by *Newbery,* and was the first of his works to which Goldsmith prefixed his name.

The comedy of "The Good-natured Man" was
1767. completed by Goldsmith early in 1767, and submitted to the perusal of Johnson, Burke, Reynolds, and others of the literary club, by whom it was heartily approved. Johnson, who was seldom half way, either in censure or applause, pronounced it the best comedy that had been written since "The Provoked Husband," and promised to furnish the prologue. This immediately became an object of great solicitude with Goldsmith, knowing the weight an introduction from the Great Cham of literature would have with the public; but circumstances occurred which he feared might drive the comedy and the prologue from Johnson's thoughts. The latter was in the habit of visiting the royal library at the Queen's (Buckingham) House, a noble collection of books, in the formation of which he had assisted the librarian, Mr. Bernard, with his advice. One evening, as he was seated there by the fire reading, he was surprised by the entrance of the King (George III.), then a young man, who sought this occasion to have a conversation with him. The

conversation was varied and discursive, the King shifting from subject to subject according to his wont. "During the whole interview," says Boswell, "Johnson talked to His Majesty with profound respect, but still in his open, manly manner, with a sonorous voice, and never in that subdued tone which is commonly used at a levee and in the drawing-room. 'I found His Majesty wished I should talk,' said he, 'and I made it my business to talk. I find it does a man good to be talked to by his sovereign. In the first place, a man cannot be in a passion.'" It would have been as well for Johnson's colloquial disputants could he have often been under such decorous restraint. Profoundly monarchical in his principles, he retired from the interview highly gratified with the conversation of the King and with his gracious behaviour. "Sir," said he to the librarian, "they may talk of the King as they will, but he is the finest gentleman I have ever seen." "Sir," said he subsequently to Bennet Langton, "his manners are those of as fine a gentleman as we may suppose Louis the Fourteenth or Charles the Second."

Goldsmith's connexion with Newbery, the bookseller, now led him into a variety of temporary jobs, such as a pamphlet on the Cock Lane ghost, a "Life of Beau Nash," the famous master of ceremonies at Bath, etc. One of the best things for his fame, however, was the remodelling and republication of his "Chinese Letters," under the title of "The Citizen of the World," a work which has long since taken its merited stand among the classics of the English language. "Few works," it has been observed by one of his biographers, "exhibit a nicer perception or more delicate delineation of life and manners. Wit, humour, and sentiment pervade every page; the vices and follies of the day are touched with the most playful and diverting satire; and English characteristics, in endless variety, are hit off with the pencil of the master."

The busy hand and active brain of John Newbery were soon to be quieted for ever; in the zenith of his fame and prosperity he was overtaken by death. His son Francis was summoned from Oxford, in the 1767. latter part of 1767, to London, in consequence of his father's severe illness. He declined gradually and sank under his complaint on the 22nd of December following, at the comparatively early age of fifty-four, and was buried, by his own request, in the churchyard at his birthplace, in Waltham St. Lawrence, and upon his tomb is the following epitaph by the Rev. C. Hunter :—

> " Stay, passenger, and contemplate
> Virtues, which arose on this spot :
> Urbanity, that adorned society,
> Knowledge, that instructed it,
> Industry, that raised a family to affluence,
> Sagacity, that discerned, and
> Skill, that introduced

The most powerful discovery
In the annals of medicine.

The humble wisdom that taught,
And still teaches, moral lessons
To the rising generation.

Lament! that a breath inspired
With such virtues is sunk in dust.
Rejoice! that, through Christ,
It is immortal!"

Few men have died more generally or more sincerely lamented; all the newspapers of the time spontaneously burst forth in expressions of commendation of his character, of regret at his loss, which was considered premature. He ranked among his friends men of the first literary and artistic talent.

Washington Irving, referring to John Newbery's death, speaks of him as "Goldsmith's old friend, though frugal-handed employer of picture book renown." The poet has celebrated him as the friend of all mankind, who coined the brains of authors in the times of their exigency. Every other record of him we have been able to find speaks of him as "honest John Newbery"; which, having been so often applied to him, seems to have been in every way well merited. He was, no doubt, a keen man of business, cautious in all his doings, and able to make a good bargain.

History informs us that so generous had John Newbery been to Oliver Goldsmith that when the former died the latter owed him £200.

Francis Newbery was advised by Dr. James, Dr. Johnson, and the rest of his friends to quit his medical studies, and carry on his late father's business, and he acted accordingly. He had so far advanced during his five or six years' residence at Oxford and Cambridge, attending lectures on anatomy and chemistry, medicine as well as the classics, and preparing subjects for John Hunter, the celebrated anatomist, whose pupil he became, that but for the event of his father's death in 1767, he had thought of preparing for his first medical degree.

Francis Newbery, his son, was passionately addicted to the violin, and spent much time in private musical parties, to the detriment of his studies at the two universities. Dr. Johnson seriously affronted him by telling him that he had better give his fiddle to the first beggar-man he met, and subsequently defended himself by the assertion that the time necessary to acquire a competent skill on a musical instrument must interfere with his pursuit of the profession of physic, which required great application and multifarious knowledge.

1770. An important year was 1770, when Francis Newbery, at St. James' Church, Bath, married Mary Raikes, the only sister of Robert Raikes, of Sunday-school fame, and proprietor of the *Gloucester Journal.* In the Thames Embankment Gardens, adjoining Cleopatra's Needle, the Sunday-schools of Great Britain erected his statue in bronze.

MARY NEWBERY, *née* RAIKES, born 1747, died 1829.
From the family portrait by Romney.

For this 5,100 guineas was paid in May, 1909.

Dr. Robert James, of Bruton Street, sent greetings, having petitioned and humbly represented to His most excellent Majesty, King George III., that he had invented an analeptic pill for rheumatism, etc.,

1775. on January 24th, 1775. This patent was granted, and concludes, "In witness whereof we have caused these our letters to be made patent. Witness OURSELF, at Westminster, the 25th day of November, in the 15th year of our reign." This patent was petitioned for, and taken out, as stated in the parchment, "for restraining several extravagant and unwarrantable practices." These patents, each having the great seal attached and secured in the original leather-covered boxes, have been handed down safely to the present day.

This was evidently a valuable property, as this provision shows, and for the true performance of all and singular, the covenants and agreements hereinafter contained, each party doth bind himself to the other in the special sum of £10,000.

1777. On March 7th in this year Francis Newbery became a citizen of London, and purchased his freedom of the Goldsmiths' Company, beginning the associations his family have continued with both for 143 years.

Of his third son (number 5 on the list of his children), born May 29th, 1777, his mother wrote in her "Memoirs" "Francis entered the army in March, 1794." He rose through the various grades to that of a lieutenant-general in 1830. In 1842 he received the colonelcy of the 3rd Dragoon Guards, acted in Ireland during the rebellion of 1798, was present at the engagement with the rebels and the French at Ballinamuck. In 1816 he commanded the cavalry brigade at the siege and capture of Huttrus. Again, in 1817 and 1818, he superintended the proceedings of the cavalry of the left division of the Marquis of Hastings' gallant army, which was the first engaged with the Pindarees, taking the whole of their baggage and camp. He was subsequently removed to the command of the cavalry, with a light division, under Major-General Sir Thomas Brown, captured at one fort nine pieces of artillery and took prisoner the artillery general ; he was afterwards present at several severe and successful attacks on the enemy's troops. The whole period of General Newbery's service comprised fifty-three years. This gallant veteran died at Wiesbaden, in 1847, aged 70.

1779. The removal from the corner of Ludgate Hill to 45, St. Paul's Churchyard, in 1779, gave more scope for the increasing business. A little house-warming was given in honour of the occasion, and a few friends were invited, Dr. Johnson being one of the party. It is on record that on this occasion the famous littérateur "was in high good humour, and rendered himself extremely agreeable to the company." He also expressed much satisfaction on finding that the business had produced so

46

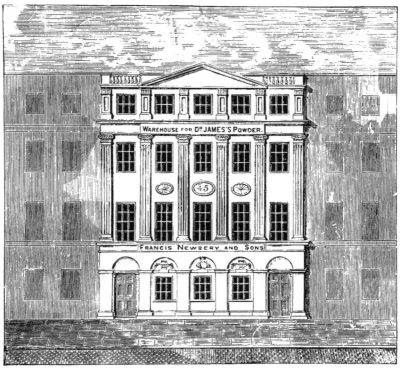

WAREHOUSE for Dᴿ JAMES'S POWDER.

45

FRANCIS NEWBERY AND SONS

45, St. Paul's Churchyard,
where Dr. Johnson was entertained in 1779.

good an establishment as this newly-built freehold house.

"Sir," said Dr. Johnson, "it could not be wrong; the only difficulty was that of detaching your mind from literary occupations and relinquishing the profession of medicine. You had the good sense to surmount it, and now, after having had the education you are enabled, by your father's industry and your own, to lead the life of a gentleman." "This little "speech of the great lexicographer was made to "Francis Newbery, who was a scholar, and a poet, " and also a lover of music," according to John Taylor, in the *Records of my Life.* "I became acquainted "with him through the medium of my friend, Sir "Francis Freeling, first Baronet, Secretary of the " General Post Office, who married his eldest daughter, "and a more pleasant, unaffected and intelligent lady " I never knew."

The copy preserved of the *Universal Daily*
1786. *Register,* of July 1st, 1786, price threepence, shows the red halfpenny revenue stamp, and contains, *inter alia,* Sketch of a petit Maitre Venson, by William Cooper, Esq., of the Inner Temple, of 24 lines, commencing, "Venerate the man whose heart is warm," &c.

The articles of agreement respecting the *London*
1787. *Chronicle* under date July 7th, 1787, in the 27th year of George III., show there were ten partners, of whom Francis Newbery, Michael Power, his

brother-in-law, and Mary Power (*née* Newbery) have been referred to previously. The ten signatures are affixed. The condition of this instrument is perfect and fresh, notwithstanding its age of 122 years.

In No. 3178 of the *Morning Herald*, Tuesday, 1790. December 28th, 1790, price fourpence, red halfpenny stamp included, is the following extract from a letter, signed Jenny Sarcasm, to the editor, on "The Rights of Women," a topic interesting nearly 120 years ago :—

"Women, Sir, have rights, and the time will "come when the answerers of Burke (I'm told they "are all Bachelors, or Old Maids) shall be ashamed "of themselves, and view us with the gallant eyes "of a Burke just rising above the horizon. My "brother Sam says, we have more rights than we "know what to do with."

These chronicles, dialogues, extracts, quotations, periodicals, agreements, and the matrimonial creed, commencing in the *Morning Herald* of December 28th, 1790, are in good preservation.

The first and third sons of Francis and Mary Newbery are mentioned in Stapleton's Eton lists, 1791. under the year 1791 :—"Newbery, ma., John, of Hereford Street, colonel in the army, died 1854, aged 80. Newbery, mi., Francis, lieut.-general— colonel 3rd Dragoon Guards, died at Wiesbaden, 1849. Both were oppidans. These were the father and uncle of the elder, and grandfather and great uncle of the younger, directors of the present firm."

From the family Portrait of Col. JOHN NEWBERY,
painted 1838 by Jno. Prescott Knight, R.A., and exhibited in
the Royal Academy. Born 1774, died 1854.

1795.   Francis Newbery purchased Heathfield House and Park, in Sussex, was pricked for High Sheriff by the King, and entertained His Majesty's judges.

1798.   He succeeded his father on his death in 1767, was an ardent sportsman, with his gun, as well as with the hounds, and his shooting propensities, like other men's hobby-horses, became naturally the occasion of jocular remarks. It happened that at one of the meetings of the lovers of our immortal bard, at the Shakespeare Tavern, for the purpose of encouraging Alderman Boydell in the undertaking of a grand edition of his plays, our sportsman was absent. Enquiry was made by the rest of the party, when one, who had more hesitation in words than in wit, and who was too fond of humour to suffer an opportunity for a good quiz to escape, informed them that his friend Newbery had heard of a woo-woo-woo-woodcock in his park at Heathfield, Sussex, and had taken a po-po-post-chaise and four, and had gone after it. Sir Joshua Reynolds was struck with the story, and at the next meeting, in all the simplicity of his nature, enquired if it were true.

THE RETURN TO HEATHFIELD PARK
By Francis Newbery.

Hail! all the dear delights once more;
    That cheer thy rude domain.
What joy! thy sylvan haunts t'explore,
    Thy beauties to regain!

The bold blue hills majestic line :—
   The plains, the distant sea,
Deep glens, and woods, and lawns combine
   In richest harmony.

But the lov'd scenes we here descry
   A latent spell impart,
And, while they lure the wond'ring eye,
   Arrest the captive heart.

The sweet enchantress, then, we'll own,
   Whose charms our breast inspire,
'Tis Nature ! Nature's self alone !
   In all her wild attire !

These stanzas were set in a beautiful glee by Dr. Crotch.

1804.   The monthly army list, December, 1804, page 52, has under Sussex 48, Col. the Duke of Richmond, Lieut.-Col. Lord Pelham, Majors Sir Chas. Burrell, Bart., and John Newbery, August 11th, 1803. Forty-four brother officers' names follow. The Duke being ordered to the continent in those days of war, John Newbery, Francis Newbery's eldest son, mentioned above, was promoted to the command of his regiment.

1806.   A rare engraving, dated January 6th, 1806, comprising the West Front of St. Paul's Cathedral, Lord Nelson's funeral cortège, the Newberys' house of business, showing their name, and the windows and roof crowded with people, is preserved in their counting house.

1818.   Francis Newbery died in 1818, and was buried, with his wife and some of their eleven children, in the

LORD NELSON'S FUNERAL CORTÈGE PASSING NEWBERY'S PREMISES (ON EXTREME LEFT OF PICTURE), 6TH JAN., 1806.

family vault under the chancel of Heathfield Church, and was succeeded by his eldest son, John, who was born in 1774, educated at Eton, and St. John's College, Cambridge. Under his management, with his brother William, the business steadily went on for thirty-six years, until 1854, without much change. Things went smoothly in those days : competition was not felt. Little mention has been made of him. The part he took was never a very active one ; the control and management were comparatively easy. He spent more time at the Senior United Service Club, Pall Mall, in the congenial society of his brother officers, than in St. Paul's Churchyard at the business house.

The concern, and all commercial establishments, had not to contend with the opposition now prevalent. Those were quiet times. It was not then so difficult to keep to the front, and pushing was not so necessary.

The truth was, his mind was not emancipated from the pursuit of knowledge which distinguished his young manhood at Eton and Cambridge. His necessities were not so great as to make an exclusive application to business imperative. He joined what a sarcastic barrister has called "the ranks of the gentlemen who are not anxious for business." All he needed came to him. He appeared to be too much of a scholar and military man to assume readily the habit of an adroit man of business, and, though the eldest, lived to be the last of Francis Newbery's eight sons, and the only one of them who figures in these reminiscences. John Newbery was, upon the nomination of the Earl of Chichester, appointed an Inspector of ship letters, General Post Office, London, on February 22nd, 1816, which office he resigned in 1830.

In 1848, through interest with the directors of the Honourable East India Company, Henry Charles Le Blanc Newbery, his eldest son, had a commission given him, was gazetted ensign in the 51st Madras Native Infantry, and sailed in the *Devonshire* to India. His father bade him adieu on board.

Henry was fourteen years with his regiment in India, before and after 1857, the mutiny year, and at the close of his seventeen years' service, including three years' furlough, having attained captain's rank, his life was suddenly cut short by the falling of a wall at Paddington a few days before his return to the East. In Emmanuel Church, Maida Hill, his brother officers erected a marble tablet to his memory. He died May 16th, 1865, aged 34.

1834.	Arthur Le Blanc Newbery's life dates from 1834. He and his three brothers enjoyed the advantage of a resident private tutor, an M.A. of Oxford.

A. Le Blanc Newbery commenced his oversea adventures by joining his father's and mother's friends, who were, with their seven sons, going to Victoria, Australia, on board the 800-ton East

Captain Henry Charles Le Blanc Newbery,
51st Madras Native Infantry.
Born December 2nd, 1831.   Killed May 16th, 1865.
Aged 34.

Indiaman, *Koh-i-noor*, for a three months' sail to the southern hemisphere on November 9th, 1852. Arriving at Melbourne in February, 1853, he engaged with a squatter who owned a sheep and cattle station in the Upper Pyrenees, carrying 30,000 sheep and 3,000 wild cattle 180 miles up the country to join his staff. His walk, accompanied by a bullock dray, team of six bullocks, the driver, and a Lancashire lad, occupied three weeks. All sleeping was done on the ground, mostly under a wagon sheet stretched over the pole of the vehicle which conveyed stores. When the rain poured, as a black fellow called it, "Big one rain," a trench had to be dug to carry off the water. The goldfields at Ballarat, Buninyong, etc., at that time were exciting great interest, but not being close to the road were not visited. The track to the station was mostly the natural turf. Seven to ten miles a day became the usual rate of travelling, and camping at sunset was arranged where good feed was abundant. The bullocks had splendid memories, for if during the day they came across food they liked, they would go back to it when they were unyoked, and the party asleep, though they were hobbled to make a stroll difficult, and hours were spent perhaps in finding them, sometimes days. Upon the ring-leader's neck would be fastened a bell to show where he was and where the others were likely to be.

A few miles from the station A. Le B. Newbery's

boots gave way, and some he bought to complete the walk lamed him, so that he did not come off with flying colours on arrival. Soon after, to prove his value and test his ability to grow into a bushman by finding his way to unknown and little-frequented places, by desire he undertook a mission of nine or ten miles through the wild bush to the hut of two Chinese shepherds, who had each charge of 1,000 sheep. Our new bushman, before starting, was assured that there was a track to John Bull's hut, but so few took that direction that it was not found, because there was none. In those early days of the colony that was serious. Skeletons were found of wayfarers in the forests at the foot of giant eucalyptus trees, with initials cut in the bark of those who, while prospecting, lost their lives. In 1853 his first distance bush raid alone might have ended disastrously and been his last; he lost his way, his bearings, nearly his courage, and found himself, as sailors say, on his beam ends.

But he was watched; so, not having yet learned how to speak to God, being so ignorant, as the drizzle came down he knelt and prayed, "Lord, show me the way," being then quite a stranger to his God, Who answered his poor petition in *two ways*—by leading him, after a couple of hours' further walk, to the very place he was sent to, and by showing him the way to Himself, and not a word of reproof for *not coming sooner* or not behaving

THE AUSTRALIAN BUSH SURROUNDINGS OF ARTHUR LE BLANC NEWBERY, IN 1853.

better! That memorable day he can never forget! This poor man cried, and the Lord heard him, and delivered him out of all his troubles. From his Melbourne, St. Kilda, Collingwood, and Prahran life he took the ride, occupying a week, of 175 miles, accompanied by two men and four horses, to Glencarty, the Macartneys', his cousins, cattle station; he made a pen and ink sketch of their bush house, which he retains as a memento of their hospitality in 1856. The members composing this up-country riding party used their saddles as pillows, removed their spurs, and rolled themselves in blankets to protect them from the frost and ice. The dryest spot that could be found by the roadside became the ground bedplace, near to the burning embers, provided they had tinder, flint and steel, dry twigs, and leaves or grass. So hard put to it were the riders that sometimes water in the clay impression of a horse's hoof, dipped up in a tin pannikin and boiled, made their tea. Through the interest of his cousin, the Dean of Melbourne, he enjoyed a position in the house of Messrs. Raleigh, Loche, Thorpe & Co., at Melbourne, and received a testimonial.

A. Le Blanc Newbery once rode with saddle-bags, scales and weights, and banknotes, to buy gold-dust from the miners at the McIvor goldfields. This was a healthful outing in a new neighbourhood, beyond Heathcote.

ARTHUR LE BLANC NEWBERY, born 1834.

visit had limits, for he had to be at Pointe de Galle to catch the mail steamer to Aden in a few days. His return to Palamcottah—ninety miles—and bidding good-bye during this peep among military customs and officers, moved him back to Tuticorin, *en route* to Ceylon. The Madras Presidency was loyal during the Mutiny which raged in Bengal in 1857.

His native servant, Abdul Khader, was of great service; he brought the bandy wallahs to reason, when on the journey to and fro they were obstreperous and exacting, tardy and forgetful. This journey by bullock bandy was 256 miles, and full of interest.

The Tappal wallahs of 1858 answered the description in Jer. li. 31 exactly: "One post shall run to meet another, and one messenger to meet another." The time occupied in conveying a letter or Banghy Post parcel from Tinnevelly to Tuticorin in 1858 (Henry C. Le Blanc Newbery used to post a loaf every week to a brother officer at Ramnad) was fixed by the time it took for a man to run a certain distance, give over his load to another, who ran another section, and so on until the mileage was covered and the mails delivered. The mail steamer *Emeu* calling at Pointe de Galle, Arthur Newbery steamed to Aden, thence into the Red Sea, which is 1,250 miles long, across the Isthmus of Suez via Cairo to Alexandria by the Pasha of Egypt's Railway, crossing the Nile three times; took the next steamer to Malta, through Gibraltar on board the *Cambria*, leaving Pompey's Pillar and Cleopatra's Needle on the beach at Alexandria, and so on safely to Southampton.

Having spent several years in the far East, in travel, and business life in one of the chief commercial houses in Melbourne, Australia, he returned to England, visiting South India and Ceylon on his way to Southampton, in 1858—the year after the mutiny—taking a share in the management of the business, the whole of which had devolved upon his younger brother Lionel, after their father's death in 1854. Arthur Newbery married in 1867, and has children and grandchildren.

In Australia he commenced, and on his return home, was permitted to continue for more than half a century his testimony for God in Sunday Schools. During several happy years his sisters and brother were working with him in the same school. To the number of seven the Newberys kept together in holding the attention of the scholars to their Bibles and to God.

His younger brother, Alfred, who had received through his mother's cousin, Captain Milne, R.N., Junior Lord of the Admiralty, a nomination for a naval cadetship, and had come from London with his father and brother, ascended the gangway of the *Victory* (to the deck of which his father was hoisted from her yard-arm), to pass his preliminary examination for the navy in 1848.

LIONEL NEWBERY, born 1837, died 1910.

FRANCIS RAIKES LE BLANC NEWBERY,
born 1870.

His first appointment was to H.M.S. *Powerful* (80 guns), then to H.M.S. *Fisguard*, guardship in the Thames, serving afterwards on board the *Leander* (50 guns), in the Mediterranean Squadron, under Captain Dacres, R.N.

For their service abroad relatives made Henry and Alfred presents, etc., and in their uniforms they attended divine service as a part of their send-off.

1837.　Lionel Newbery learnt business habits in the counting house of Boyd & Co., Ceylon Merchants, in the City of London, and gradually worked into the family concern of the Newbery's, crossed the Atlantic twice, travelled on the continent, married in 1867, he was diligent in business, was much interested in charitable and philanthropic work, and died, aged 73, in August, 1910, lamented by his widow, two sons, and two daughters, and many others.

On his father's death, he commenced his reign of fifty-five years, unbroken and steady of purpose, through the blessings of God, and had as his partner, from 1858, his elder brother, Arthur.

Between Arthur and Lionel the blood relationship, the deed of partnership, and their being brothers-in-law, linked them together in a three-fold bond.

1870.　Francis R. Le Blanc Newbery was born 1870, is the second son of Lionel Newbery, and like his two brothers was educated at Dulwich College, under Dr. Carver and Bishop Welldon. His two brothers,

Archibald and Herbert, graduated at Cambridge University, proceeding after ordination to India. Francis Newbery entered the business about 1888, taking up the freedom of the City and the Goldsmiths' Company in April, 1901. He joined the Barnet Lodge of Freemasons. His travels have not been beyond the confines of Europe.

1872. Percy Le Blanc Newbery, born 1872, the elder twin son of Arthur Newbery, aforesaid, spent several years in the United States and Canada. Is a freeman of the Goldsmiths' Company and of the City of London. He, and his cousin Frank, are shaping their courses to sustain the prestige handed down to them by their ancestors.

The sixth generation of Newberys are the grandchildren of Arthur and Lionel, besides nephews and nieces, who are numerous and their ages various.

This account would be very deficient if the devotion of Messrs. Edward and Frederick Pickering, and many others, was not mentioned. To their persistent, steady unflagging business capacity, given to the best interests of the house, is owing in a large degree its growth and development during a long course of years. Such valuable gentlemen are the backbone and stay of a commercial house; they have grown up in it, and with its fortunes their best energies have been linked.

Three of the Directors of the new company, which was incorporated in 1904, are, as their

PERCY LE BLANC NEWBERY, born 1872.

ancestors were before them, liverymen of one of the City companies—the Goldsmiths'—which has had the name Newbery on its rolls for two hundred and forty years. The crest, coat of arms, and the motto (Si Recte Perstes) are on the stained glass windows of the dining hall.

Dates of taking up of the Freedom and Livery of the Goldsmiths' Company by the Newbery Family.

William Newbery	...	...18th Dec., 1663
William Newbery	...	...30th June, 1686
Francis Newbery	...	... 9th April, 1777
John Newbery...	...	... 7th Mar., 1804
Robert Newbery	...	... 6th Feb., 1805
Charles Newbery, on the Court		4th Mar., 1807
Thomas Raikes Newbery	...	4th Mar., 1807
William Newbery	...	... 5th Aug., 1818
Arthur Le Blanc Newbery	...	2nd May, 1866,*1872
Lionel Newbery	...	... 2nd May, 1866,*1874
Francis R. Le Blanc Newbery		6th May, 1891,*1905
Percy Le Blanc Newbery	...	3rd July, 1894
Rev. Lionel A. McClintock Newbery, M.A. ...		... 4th Nov., 1896
Rev.Herbert E.L.Newbery,M.A.		5th Dec., 1900

* On the Livery.

At the present time, the house in St. Paul's Churchyard, on the site of the original establishment, on the N.W. corner of Ludgate Hill, carries on its fascia, carved in stone, life-size medallions of John

Newbery's, Dr. Johnson's and Oliver Goldsmith's faces. Their names were gilded, but time has nearly obliterated them.

The stone sign of "The Bible and Sun," referred to in the advertisements in the *London Chronicle* of 1759, is built into the front, above the coping stone, and bears the inscription, FIAT LUX. "Let there be Light." This remains to-day.

THE HOUSE OF NEWBERY.

JOHN NEWBERY.

	Born.	Years.	A.D.	Died.
JOHN NEWBERY	... 1713	... 21	from 1746	to 1767

FRANCIS NEWBERY & SONS.

	Born.	Years.	A.D.	Died.
FRANCIS NEWBERY	... 1743	... 51	from 1767	to 1818
JOHN NEWBERY	... 1774	... 36	,, 1818	,, 1854
*LIONEL NEWBERY	... 1837	... 56	,, 1854	,,
*ARTHUR NEWBERY	... 1834	... 52	,, 1858	,,
†FRANCIS NEWBERY, jun.	1870	... 22	,, 1888	,,
†PERCY NEWBERY	... 1872	... 11	,, 1899	,,

A.D. D.G., 1746 to 1910 = 164 years, *de die in diem.*

* Managing Directors Limited Co.   † Junior Directors Limited Co.

It is noteworthy in these days of development and change that in the 164 years of this house there has been always one Newbery, sometimes two, and to-day, 1910, there are four active Newberys.

Thus the business of the 18th, 19th, and 20th centuries commenced, was built up and continued during six generations by God's favour and blessing.

LAUS DEO.

ERNEST BARRY NEWBERY, born 1902.
Son of Ernest Arthur Newbery, L.D.S., R.C.S.Eng.,
and Grandson of A. Le Blanc Newbery.

ROBERT RAIKES, of Gloucester.
Born September 14th, 1735, died April 5th, 1811.

A good many pages having been devoted to the history of the Newberys of Waltham St. Lawrence, Berkshire, and later of Heathfield, Sussex, in three generations, mention must now be made of the manner in which the Raikes of Gloucester, the Irish McClintocks, the Le Blancs of Chelsea and elsewhere, became allied to them in marriage, showing how the remaining three generations under review came into being.

The Rev. Robert Raikes (to go no further back into the remote past), Vicar of Holderness, in Yorkshire, was born *circa* 1685, and died September 7th, 1757.

Robert Raikes, his son, who established in 1722 one of the six oldest established county newspapers, and was the proprietor and editor of *The Gloucester Journal*, married the daughter of the Rev. Richard Drew.

Their son, Robert Raikes, first saw the light in the house in Palace yard, just beneath the shadow of Gloucester Cathedral, September 14th, 1735, and inherited the large and important property of his father. Anne, his wife, was daughter of Thomas Trigge, of Newnham, Gloucester, whom he married in 1767 at St. James's Church, London. She had two brothers, Sir Thomas Trigge and Admiral Trigge. Robert and Anne Raikes were blessed with a family. In a letter to a friend in 1787, he spoke of their children as six excellent girls and two lovely boys. They named the eldest Robert Napier, born November 3rd, 1783, who became a clergyman, adorned his sacred calling by an exemplary life, and married, as his helpmeet, the daughter of the Venerable Archdeacon Probyn. Their second son was Richard Raikes, M.A., of Cambridge, who married Miss Mee.

The Rev. Robert Napier Raikes's son was born at Drayton, October 13th, 1813, where his father was vicar, and was named after him, Robert Napier. He often met his grandfather among his Sunday scholars, and had five brothers, all of whom (except one, who joined the Civil Service) entered the Indian Army, under the Honourable East India Company. Robert Napier Raikes, being at Addiscombe in 1828 as a military cadet, wore the uniform of the period—a swallow-tailed coat, with a high stock—was expelled for refusing to give the names of five cadets who were out one night without leave. However, for him, this was not serious, since several of his family were connected with the military authorities, so he got his commission, November 19th, 1829, as ensign in the Bengal Army. Sailing from Portsmouth on November 29th, and landing at Calcutta on May 14th, 1830, it took him till November 7th to reach his regiment at Cawnpore, after nearly a year's travelling. His men carried the old flint-lock musket, of which Wellington's maxim was, "Don't fire until you see the whites of their eyes."

It was thirty-five years before he came home

GENERAL ROBERT NAPIER RAIKES,
Indian Army.
Born October 13th, 1813. Died March, 1909. Aged 96.

on furlough. His wife was the daughter of Major Beckett; she stood by him all through the Mutiny in 1857, and before and after several children were born to them. Serving with the 67th Bengal Native Infantry, he was appointed Adjutant to the famous native Grenadiers; later, to the same rank in the First Gwalior Cavalry. Being a good linguist, having picked up all the dialects, able to speak one at one place and another ten miles away, while he was Major, he managed to gather the whole of the treasury at Mynpoorie, 20,000 rupees in all, and sent it into Agra by two loyal Sikhs, marching his men to within ten miles of that city. They quoted a native proverb, that "an ill-wind was blowing," and refused to go any further. There was no mutiny; they just disbanded themselves and went home. Being devoted to him, as he rode away they formed up on each side of the road, with tears pouring down their faces, and bade him farewell. Several of those men who deserted came to him at Calcutta and begged permission to rejoin the army.

He wore the Burmah and Gwalior medals, retired with the rank of General, was called the "father of the army," had served in some deadly spots, and knew a regiment which was commanded by the junior lieutenant, because all the other officers were sick. He killed a hundred tigers, and thought nothing of riding that number of miles to keep an engagement and then riding back to his quarters.

His cousin, A. Le Blanc Newbery, to the last corresponded with him, and his letters had an interest all their own. He, aged ninety-six, and his widow, aged seventy-five, died within a week of each other, at Eastbourne, in March, 1909, leaving four sons and two daughters. Their parents were buried at Longhope, in Gloucestershire. He and his brother, Rev. Richard Raikes, were the grandsons of Robert Raikes, as Arthur and Lionel Newbery and their sister Laura are the grandchildren of his sister, Mary Raikes.

As early as 1720 a gleam of light began to show itself in the city of Gloucester. The streets were unpaved, locomotion was slow, "the flying coaches" took two or three days in the journey to London ; religion seemed to have died out. George Whitefield, afterwards the great preacher, was known there as a young thief, who thought he atoned for his thefts by bestowing some of his gains upon those poorer than himself. While he was studying for Holy Orders, reports state that he deposited some of his writings in Raikes's *Gloucester Journal* letter-box.

Thomas Raikes, on December 8th, 1774, married at St. George's Church, Bloomsbury, London, Charlotte, daughter of the Hon. Henry Finch, youngest son of Daniel, Earl of Winchelsea. This Thomas Raikes was a London merchant, governor of the Bank of England during the crisis in 1797, and a personal friend of Wilberforce and the younger William Pitt.

1735.　　Robert Raikes, born 1735, who, if not the originator of our Sunday Schools, as he has been called, by his persistent labours and in his editorial capacity, since his *Journal* teemed with notices of new schools, was associated with their establishment in 1780, giving testimonies of their value. The Rev. John Berrington wrote, "Robert Raikes first proposed and realised the scheme of Sunday Schools.". One speedy result of their institution was the almost total suppression of Sunday revelling and wakes throughout the country.

His spirit was moved in him by the surrounding ignorance and wretchedness of the people. "Ah! sir," said a woman to him, "could you take a view of this part of the town on Sunday, you would be shocked indeed!" He asked her if there were any decent, well-disposed women who kept schools for teaching to read. So he arranged to pay some of them to instruct those he collected in the Bible and Church Catechism, giving them a shilling for their day's employment.

The paper duty and the advertisement tax made it a hard struggle for the appearance of the first number of the *Gloucester Journal* on April 9th, 1722. The journals, too, of the House of Commons in 1728, and again in 1729, took exception to references Raikes made in his columns to the debates, and he was summoned to appear at the Bar of the House in consequence.

Howard, the philanthropist, visiting Gloucester in 1773, was entertained by Robert Raikes, and inspected the gaols and exposed the abuses committed upon the prisoners, some of whom would have been starved to death but for the humanity of the felons.

Admirers of Raikes rest his claim to the honoured title of "founder of Sunday Schools." There can be no doubt that his labours were the direct sequence of his philanthropic work in the Gloucester gaols. He was called the father of the poor. In his intercourse with these wretched delinquents he saw their profound ignorance, utter contempt of wholesome restraints, and disregard of the sacred duties of religion. Had the children been disposed to learn or attend to anything that was good, their parents were neither able nor willing to teach or direct them. They were, therefore, a perpetual nuisance to the sober part of the community. The foundation, he well knew, must be laid in the fear and love of God, in a reverence for all things relating to the Divine honour and service. The neglected state of the juveniles was one of the most alarming evils of the day. Very few received the benefit of any education. Profane, filthy, and disorderly, are descriptions which Raikes gives of the children he saw around him, and as were they, so were the parents. It was with this deplorable state of things that he set himself to grapple. The Bishop of Gloucester, at his visitation in July, 1786, said he doubted not that, with proper management and under the inspection of the parochial clergy, Sunday Schools might be productive of great good among the children throughout his diocese.

No sooner had Raikes called attention to his scheme, than good men and women far and wide began to adopt it. The poet Cowper declared that he knew no nobler means by which the reformation of the poorer classes could be effected.

The distinctive character of Raikes's endeavour lies in the fact that, having in common with several other kindred spirits perceived the advantages that would attend Sunday teaching, he did not content himself, as some did, with establishing a school or schools in his own neighbourhood, but, by means of his newspaper and other organs of public opinion, recommended the practice far and wide, and never ceased its advocacy till the scheme was generally adopted throughout the land. The movement, hitherto unheard of save in a few provincial towns and villages, was now brought into the light of day. In vigorous language he introduced it to all classes of readers—from cottage to king, all learned of the new institution. He attempted to raise Sunday teaching of the Bible into a universal system. Finding the practice local, he endeavoured to make it national.

The mainspring of his life and heart was right. He loved God, and therefore he loved the children, remembering that the Good Shepherd had said, "Feed My lambs."

Adam Smith, according to one of Raikes's letters in 1787, declared that no plan so simple and promising, with equal ease and simplicity, for the improvement of manners, had been devised since the days of the Apostles.

At Christmas in that year George III. and Queen Charlotte invited Raikes to an interview. They graciously visited a Sunday school, and when, in 1788, the King visited Cheltenham, the Queen commanded Miss Burney to take an airing at Gloucester, who described Raikes as a very principal man in all benevolent institutions, and how he and Mrs. Raikes received her with open arms.

John Wesley wrote this first notice of Sunday Schools on July 18th, 1784: "I find these schools springing up wherever I go. Perhaps God may have a deeper end therein than men are aware of. Who knows but some of these schools may become nurseries for Christians."

In 1788 he wrote: "The spirit in which the trebles, boys and girls, sang at Bolton in the Sunday school so suits the melody that I defy anything to exceed it, except the singing of the angels in our Father's house."

Writing in 1787, Richard Rodda expressed his belief that these schools will be one great means of reviving religion throughout the kingdom; and in

1788 he said, "I verily believe these schools are one of the noblest specimens of charity which have been set on foot since the days of William the Conqueror."

Visiting relations at Windsor in 1787, Robert Raikes had the honour of introducing his institution to *Queen Charlotte*, who sent for him to know by what accident a thought which promised so much benefit as the Sunday Schools was suggested to his mind, and what effects were observable in consequence on the manners of the poor. The conversation lasted more than an hour. Her Majesty most graciously said she envied those who had this power of doing good, and personally promoting the welfare of society by giving such instruction, a pleasure from which, by her position, she was debarred. It is impossible to do justice to the charming manner in which the Queen expressed the most benevolent sentiments and the tenderest regard for the happiness of the poor. Hannah More endeavoured to enlighten her neighbours by means of a Sunday school in 1789, and found every house a scene of the greatest ignorance and vice. She saw but one Bible in all the parish, and that was used to prop a flower-pot. In five years' time she had in regular attendance two hundred children and two hundred adult scholars.

We always discover it is more blessed to give than to receive, so we find that Robert Raikes never regretted his self-denying labour for the children.

It became the very joy of his heart and life. He said: "What a wide and extensive field of rational enjoyment opens out to our view, could we allow the improvement of human nature to become a source of pleasure." The mind is happy still that is intent on good.

At the Sunday School Union, in the Old Bailey, London, is a set of tea-things, given one hundred years ago to M. Harris, which was the earliest prize given to a Sunday scholar by Robert Raikes.

As has been stated, Mary Raikes was the grand-daughter of the Rev. Robert Raikes, vicar of Holderness, in Yorkshire. Her father was his son, the second of the same name. One of their children and Robert Raikes, her brother, had business relations with Francis Newbery from 1761. During the intervening nine years the records do not give information, but her own "memoirs," extending before the date of her marriage to Francis Newbery, in 1770, till his death in 1818, being the term of their married life—forty-eight years—impart scanty information of family history, the birth of their children, their residences, marriages of some, and deaths and burial-places of others. She narrates how she came from Gloucester to Water Street on January 8th, 1770; on the 15th met Francis Newbery at Maryland Point while on a visit; returned home to Gloucester March 1st. Stayed at Bath April 26th, and she being twenty-three and Francis

Newbery twenty-seven, they were married there. The marriage settlement was made and signed by Robert Raikes; Richard Raikes, of St. John's College, Cambridge; William Raikes, of Westham, Essex, the bride's brothers; between Francis Newbery, of St. Paul's Churchyard, London, and Mary Raikes, of the Parish of St. Mary - le - Crypt, Gloucester : dated May 26th, 1770, in the tenth year of George III. The ceremony took place at St. James' Church, Bath, on May 29th, 1770. Their children were :—

(1) ELIZA, Feb. 26th, 1771.	(7) CHARLOTTE, Aug. 9th, 1781.
(2) MARY, Aug. 11th, 1772.	(8) THOMAS, April 11th, 1783.
(3) JOHN, Jan. 2nd, 1774.	(9) WILLIAM, July 31st, 1785.
(4) ROBERT, Sept. 16th, 1775.	(10) WILLIAM, July 2nd, 1788.
(5) FRANCIS, May 29th, 1777.	(11) GEORGE, Aug. 19th, 1790.
(6) CHARLES, June 5th, 1779.	

It appears that Francis Newbery took his bride to live apart from the St. Paul's house, for at No. 5, St. Paul's Churchyard, their first daughter was born. In 1772 they had a house in Aldersgate Street, where two of the children were born. This house they left in 1778, spent the holidays this summer at Addiscombe, for in 1779 they removed on August 18th into the new freehold house No. 45, St. Paul's Churchyard, which Francis Newbery built, as has been stated earlier, where Charles'—the sixth member of their family—birth took place.

Mrs. Newbery's mother, daughter of the Rev. Richard Drew, died October 30th, 1779, and in these memoirs she adds, on November 17th, "entertained Dr. Johnson," etc.

Francis Newbery went to Bristol in 1780. The riots brought him home. His mother (*née* Carnan, widow of William Carnan, proprietor and editor of the *Reading Mercury* and *Oxford Gazette*) died January 30th, 1780, aged sixty-seven. In 1782 the family took their vacation in Sussex, at Rye, etc. 1784—Francis Newbery went into Wales shooting; 1785—all went to Bexhill for seven weeks in September; 1786—visited Brighton; 1788 the family at Hastings; 1790—moved to Mincing Lane while house was repaired. An archery party in June at Addiscombe; May 28th, 1791—a family party of fifty-three, on using the new room at St. Paul's, and arrow shooting at Addiscombe. All went to Brighton. August 3rd, 1791, Mr. Newbery went to see Heathfield House and park, taking his family with him: dined with Mr. Constable, and on September 29th they took possession, eight weeks and a day after first seeing it. The place was prepared for occupation, the purchase having been concluded with Lord Heathfield, and on September 30th all the family made it their home; 1793—plays acted by the young people in the Christmas holidays to very large parties more than once. The return to Addiscombe was on January 18th; 1794—plays acted again.

Francis Newbery, junior, entered the army, May 29th, 1795. His father, Francis Newbery, High

FRANCIS NEWBERY, born 1743, died 1818.

The slopes and glades of Francis Newbery's park at Heathfield, Sussex, with a view of the house, the deer, and the church, also the sea in the distance.

(Copied from the parchment.)

"LETTERS PATENT FOR FRANCIS NEWBERY, ESQ., SHERIFF FOR THE COUNTY OF SUSSEX.

"GEORGE THE THIRD, by the Grace of God, of Great Britain, France, and Ireland, King, Defender of the Faith, and so forth.

"To Archbishops, Bishops, Dukes, Earls, Barons, Knights, Freeholders, and all others of our County of Sussex, GREETING.

"Whereas We have committed to our welbeloved Francis Newbery, Esquire, the custody of Our said County, with the appurtenances, during our pleasure, as by our Letters Patent to him hereof made more fully appeared.

"We command You, that ye be aiding, answering, and assisting, to the said Francis Newbery, as our Sheriff of our said county in all things which appertain to the said office.

"In witness whereof we have caused these Our Letters to be made Patent.

"Witness ourself, at Westminster the Eleventh Day of February, in the Thirty-fifth Year of our Reign.

"ARDEN.   SEWELL."

"GEORGE THE THIRD, by the Grace of God, of Great Britain, France, and Ireland, King, Defender of the Faith, and so forth.

"To all to whom these our Letters Patent shall come, GREETING.

"Know ye, that we have committed to our Welbeloved Francis Newbery, of Heathfield Park, Esquire, the custody of our county of Sussex, with the appurtenances, during our pleasure. So that he annually render unto US our due forms, and answer to US touching our dues, and all other matters, concerning the office of Sheriff of the county aforesaid, in OUR Court of Exchequer.

"In Witness whereof We have caused these Our letters to be made Patent.

"Witness Ourself, at Westminster, the Eleventh day of February, in the Thirty-fifth year of Our reign.

"ARDEN. SEWELL."

Sheriff (see parchments), had three assizes, went to the Levée at St. James' Palace; 1799—the Newberys became known to the Freelings, in July saw the Post Office where Francis Freeling was secretary. Francis had leave from his regiment for a short time; all went to Brighton; 1800—Freeling came to Heathfield, January 3rd. Mary married to him February 24th. August 1st all repaired to Heathfield. William Raikes died October 15th.

1801—The family at Heathfield: Francis Newbery, junior, married on September 22nd; 1802—John Newbery took leave for France, William and George greatly amusing by acting plays in the coachhouse; 1803, January 12th—Mary Martha Freeling born; John returned from France. September 17th saw Mrs. Freeling in town for the last time; 1804—Mrs. Freeling (*née* Mary Newbery) died January 8th. She was buried in the vault beneath the chancel of the church at Heathfield, the first of five Newberys interred there. The others were Francis Newbery, late of Heathfield Park in this parish, died August 7th, 1818, aged 75; Mary, his wife, died January 31st, 1829, aged 81; Mary Freeling, their eldest daughter, died January 8th, 1804, aged 32; Robert died August 13th, 1805, aged 29; Charlotte died August 24th, 1805, aged 24; also Annie Mary, daughter of Major-General Newbery, who died December 24th, 1830, aged 21 years. The parchment faculty conveying the vault from Lord

Heathfield to the Newberys in perpetuity has been preserved.

1806—John married Mary, daughter of Rev. J. Cleaver; 1811—Robert Raikes, the third, died in April, George joined the 44th Regiment; 1812—Thomas married to Miss Sutton; 1814 — George returned from Spain; 1815—George ill in Paris after Waterloo, etc.; 1817—Francis Newbery's illness began; 1818—left Heathfield for last time with him very ill, and never left his room after April 13th: on May 24th and again in June Dr. Heath administered to us all the Holy Communion, and on July 17th he departed this life, and was buried at Heathfield August 14th.

The first marriage of Colonel John Newbery, in 1806, to Mary, daughter of the Rev. James Jervis Cleaver, vicar of Holme Pierrepoint, Nottinghamshire, brought a new element into the family, which consisted of three sons and four daughters, some of whom were born at Hadley, Barnet, Herts., and others at the town house, 15, Upper Seymour Street, Portman Square, London. Several of the children and their mother, who died in 1820, were buried at Hadley.

Mrs. Francis Newbery, *née* Mary Raikes, before mentioned, left after her death, in 1829, a very interesting narration of her married life, 48 years, containing information of the births of her children, and their happy Christmas family festivities at Heathfield.

COLONEL HENRY LE BLANC,
71st Regiment.   Forty-one years Major of Chelsea Hospital.
Born 1776.   Died 1855.   Aged 79.

In the year 1829 the same third John Newbery numbered among his friends Colonel Henry Le Blanc (born 1776, died 1855, aged 79), forty-one years major of the Royal Hospital, Chelsea, and late of the 71st Regiment, whose leg was shot off in 1806 at the capture of Buenos Ayres, in the engagement under General Whitelock against the Spaniards. Colonel Le Blanc married a Miss McClintock. The third John Newbery, in 1831, chose their eldest daughter, Frances, for his second wife, thus introducing the good old Irish Protestant blood. They had four sons and three daughters. The Rev. Dr. Prideaux Lightfoot, rector of Exeter College, Oxford, vice-chancellor of that University, married Elizabeth, their second daughter. To the Rev. Tunstall Smith, rector of Wirksworth, Derbyshire, was married Lucy, the youngest. They all had families.

Sir Simon Le Blanc, born in 1748, was the second son of Thomas Le Blanc, of Charterhouse Square. In June, 1766, he was admitted a pensioner and, in the following November, elected a scholar of Trinity Hall, Cambridge. In February, 1773, he was called to the bar at the Inner Temple, and graduated LL.B. the same year. In June, 1779, he was elected fellow of his college. In June, 1799, Sir Simon was appointed puisne judge of the King's Bench and knighted. Being a consummate lawyer, he early showed his independence of mind on the Norfolk circuit. He died unmarried on April 15th, 1816, at his house in

Bedford Square, London, and was buried in the church near his Hertfordshire seat, Northaw House, Potter's Bar. This estate passed by his will to his brothers, Charles and Francis Le Blanc, who left it to Captain Thomas Edmund Le Blanc, the brother of the three brides before mentioned, all being children of Colonel Henry Le Blanc, of Chelsea Hospital, whose brother was Colonel Francis Le Blanc, of Blackbrook House, Fareham, Hants, who was born March 14th, 1790, and died January 7th, 1880, aged 90.

Their mother's relative, John McClintock, M.P., of Drumcar, co. Louth, was raised to the peerage as Lord Rathdonnell by Lord Beaconsfield.

Justice must be done, a page be found, honourable mention made of a relative who served Queen and country well. He was Admiral Sir Leopold McClintock, K.C.B., born at Dundalk in 1819, died Nov. 17th, 1907, aged 88. He entered the Royal Navy in 1831, was a cousin of the Newberys, his father was Henry McClintock (whose second son he was), his mother a daughter of Archdeacon Fleury. The first Lord Rathdonnell was his nephew. After some years of foreign service, owing to the great anxiety for the safety of Sir John Franklin and his companions—he accompanied Sir James Ross as second lieutenant on H.M.S. *Enterprise* in the Arctic Expedition in 1848, returning unsuccessful in 1849. He joined a second expedition in 1850, under Captain Austin. They

ADMIRAL SIR LEOPOLD McCLINTOCK, K.C.B.
Born 1819.   Died November 17th, 1907.
Aged 95.

were fortunate to find traces of the expedition. At Griffiths Island the ship's company were frozen up. In a remarkably plucky eighty days' sledge trip he travelled over 700 miles to the most westerly point in those Arctic wastes. He was in command, in 1852, of H.M.S. *Intrepid*—four other men-of-war formed his third searching expedition. Sir Edward Belcher was chief in command. Captain McClure and those with him were discovered, ice bound three years. McClintock travelled with sledges 1,210 miles in 105 days. Lady Franklin fitted out the 117-ton yacht *Fox*, gave him the command, and with a company of twenty-four he sailed, on July 1st, 1857, in search of her long-lost husband. They discovered a record of his death and brought home accounts of their great discoveries. Sir Leopold married in 1870, Annetta Elizabeth, second daughter of Robert Dunlop, Esq., by Anna Elizabeth, sister of the tenth Viscount Massereene, and has issue.

THE NEWBERY BUSINESS HOUSE,
CHARTERHOUSE SQUARE, LONDON, 1910.

Interesting Recollections

OF

Drs. Johnson, Oliver Goldsmith

AND

NATUS 1713.   OBIIT 1767.

John Newbery

(OF ST. PAUL'S CHURCHYARD)

Their Friend and Publisher

G I

Dr. JOHNSON, after Opie.

Interesting Recollections of Drs. Johnson, Oliver Goldsmith, and John Newbery.

SOME say it is impossible to honour too highly Dr. Johnson's memory. His friendship was sought for; to be introduced to him was esteemed a favour; a chat with him worth giving up an afternoon; his opinion in an argument carried great weight, and satisfied those who sought his advice. At Lichfield he was born, September 18th, 1709. His great mind, cramped and galled by narrow circumstances, led him to pen these lines:—

> "Has heaven reserved, in pity to the poor,
> No pathless waste, or undiscovered shore?
> No secret island in the boundless main?
> No peaceful desert yet unclaimed by Spain?
> Quick let us rise! the happy seats explore,
> And bear Oppression's insolence no more!"

Lord Chesterfield, who flattered himself that Johnson would dedicate his "Dictionary" to him, attempted to efface the feeling of coldness he had shown to its learned author, and wrote two papers in *The World* in commendation of the work. Studied compliments, finely turned, he hoped would highly delight Johnson, to whom praise, in general, was pleasing. "It must be owned" (his words were) "that our language is in a state of anarchy, and hitherto it may not have been the worse for it. The time for discrimination seems now come. Good order and authority are now necessary. But where shall we find them ? and, at the same time, the obedience due to them ? We must have recourse to the Roman expedient in times of confusion, and choose a Dictator. Upon this principle I vote for Dr. Johnson to fill that great and arduous post, and hereby declare that I make a total surrender of all my rights and privileges in the English language, as a free-born English subject, to the said Dr. Johnson ! More than this he cannot well require. His labours will very fully supply that want, and greatly contribute to the farther spreading of our language in other countries." Johnson wrote : "To be so distinguished is an honour which, being very little accustomed to favours from the great, I know not well how to receive, or in what terms to acknowledge. Is not a patron, my lord, one who looks with unconcern on a man struggling for life in the water, and when he has reached ground encumbers him with help ? The notice you have taken of my labours, had it been early, had been kind : but it has been delayed till I am indifferent, and cannot enjoy it, till I am solitary, and cannot impart it. I am unwilling the public should consider me as owing that to a patron which Providence has enabled me to do for myself. Having carried on my work thus far with so little obligation to any favourer of learning, I shall not be disappointed though I should conclude it, if less be possible, with less : for I have been long wakened from that dream of hope in which I once boasted myself with so much exultation." It is impossible to doubt that the lofty contempt, and polite, though keen, satire of Johnson, must have mortified the Earl. Dr. Warburton honoured Johnson for his manly behaviour in rejecting these condescensions. Johnson was gratified by this compliment. This took place while and when these facts became known.

Dr. Adams did his best to induce Johnson to believe that his not being received in audience by Lord Chesterfield was probably not his doing, for he had declared to Dodsley that "he would have turned off the best servant he ever had if he had known that he denied him to a man who would have been always more than welcome." In confirmation of this, he insisted on Lord Chesterfield's affability and easiness of access, especially to literary men. "Sir," said Johnson, "that's not Lord Chesterfield! He is the proudest man going!" "No," replied Dr. Adams, "there is one person, at least, as proud. I think, by your own account, you are the prouder man of the two!" "But mine," replied Johnson instantly, "was *defensive* pride." This rejoinder was one of those happy turns for which he was so remarkably ready. To show his friendliness towards this nobleman, he gave it as his opinion that "this man, I thought, had been a lord among wits, but I find he is only a wit among lords." There seems little doubt that the character of a "respectable Hottentot" in the Earl's letters was intended for Dr. Johnson.

While John Newbery's son Francis was at Merchant Taylors' School he had frequent opportunities of being in company with men of literature : with Christopher Lovatt, Dr. Hawkesworth, Dr. James, Goldsmith, and Sam. Johnson. The latter was very friendly, and his advice to the young man, who frequently visited him, was very valuable. He affronted him for seeing a violin hanging up, asked his mother to whom it belonged, who replied it was Frank's. "Then," said the Doctor, "let him give it to the first beggar man he meets, or he'll never be a scholar!" On another occasion he said : "A man always makes himself greater as he increases his knowledge."

Dr. Johnson stated that, when Akenside's "Pleasures of the Imagination" came out, he did not put his name on the poem. Rolt went to Dublin and published it under his own name. Akenside, hearing of this, vindicated his right by an edition in which this was rectified. A true author in many cases may not be able to make good his title. Johnson, from the unusual character of his writings, has bid defiance to those who endeavoured to deprive him of the credit due to his skill and learning.

> "But Shakespeare's magic could not copied be :
> Within that circle none durst walk but he."

A mother entreated Johnson to obtain the Archbishop of Canterbury's patronage for her son. His reply contained the following : "Madam, you ask me to solicit a great man, to whom I never spoke, for a young person, whom I have never seen, upon a supposition which I had no means of knowing to be true. Though he may miss the university, your son may still be wise, useful, and happy."

When Johnson was fifty-three, George III. ascended the throne ; and having been represented to His Majesty as a very learned and good man, without any certain provision, he was pleased to grant him a pension of three hundred pounds a year. Sir Joshua Reynolds had a visit from Johnson, who told him he wished to consult his friends as to the propriety of accepting this mark of favour from the King, because of the definition of *pension* and *pensioners* he had given in his "Dictionary." They satisfied him, and he waited on Lord Bute to thank him, who assured him "it was not given for anything you are to do, but for what you have done!" The fervour of gratitude prompted him to assert that the English language did not afford him terms adequate to his feelings, so he had recourse to French. "I am *pénétré* with His

Majesty's goodness." There was nothing humiliating in Johnson's acceptance of what was so unconditionally bestowed upon him.

Sir Joshua Reynolds, a Devonshire man, accompanied Dr. Johnson in 1762 on an excursion. At Plymouth the shipbuilding very much interested him. The Dockyard authorities arranged a trip to the Eddystone Lighthouse for them both. The sail was not so successful as they wished, since they were not able to land because of the rough weather. He was invited to several noblemen's estates. Dr. Amyatt, a London physician, thinking to interest him, showed him round the garden. His host asked Johnson, "Are you a botanist?" "No, sir," he replied, "I am not a botanist—am too near-sighted; should I wish to become one, I must become a reptile first."

His pension not being paid, Johnson wrote to the Earl of Bute: "Your knowledge of the world has long since taught you that every man's affairs, however little, are important to himself—every man hopes he shall escape neglect; and with reason may every man, where vices do not preclude his claim, expect favour from that beneficence which has been extended to, my lord, your lordship's much obliged and most humble servant, Sam. Johnson."

Between Johnson and Sheridan an unfortunate difference took place. To the latter a pension of two hundred pounds a year had been given, and

Johnson, thinking slightingly of Sheridan's art, exclaimed, "What, have they given *him* a pension? Then it's time for me to give up mine!" as if it were an affront to himself that a player should be rewarded like he had been. It appears that Sheridan's pension was bestowed, not because he was a player, but as a sufferer in the cause of government. He had been manager of the Theatre Royal in Ireland. Johnson afterwards said: "However, I am glad that Mr. Sheridan has a pension, for he is a very good man." But that did not soothe his injured vanity, for, in the "Life of Swift," Sheridan characterised Johnson as "a writer of gigantic fame in these days of little men."

Trinity College, Dublin, surprised Johnson with a bestowal of the academical honour of Doctor of Laws. This was in 1765. The diploma commences: "Omnibus ad quos præsenter literæ pervenerint salutem," &c.

Talking to himself was one of Johnson's habits. He frequently uttered fragments of the Lord's Prayer. His friend Davies, of whom Churchill said that he had a very pretty wife, when Johnson muttered, "Lead us not into temptation," used to whisper to Mrs. Davies, "You, my dear, are the cause of this."

"The morality of an action," said Johnson, "depends on the motive from which we act. If I fling half-a-crown to a beggar to break his head, and he picks it up and buys food with it, the effect is good physically, but my action is very wrong. So, religious exercises, if not performed to please God, avail us nothing."

Garrick having been referred to, Johnson gave him the following character: "He is the first man in the world for sprightly conversation."

Dr. Blair had been presented to Johnson at a time when the controversy concerning the Pieces published by Macpherson as translations of Ossian was at its height, and Johnson denied their authenticity. Blair asked him if he thought any man of a modern age could have written such poems. Johnson replied: "Yes, sir, many men, many women, and many children." Not knowing that Dr. Blair had published a "Dissertation," ranking them with Homer and Virgil, Johnson regretted that the subject had been introduced, and added, "I am not sorry that they got so much for their pains, Sir; it was like leading one to talk of a book when the author is concealed behind the door."

In the Cock Lane ghost scare, which gained great credit in London in 1762, many said Johnson believed, but it was found he was one of those by whom the imposture was detected. Dr. Douglas, bishop of Salisbury, examined into the matter. He was a great detector of impostures; and Johnson, in "The Gentleman's Magazine," undeceived the world.

Dr. Oliver Goldsmith got a premium at a

Dr. OLIVER GOLDSMITH,
after Sir Joshua Reynolds.

Christmas examination in Trinity College, Dublin. A premium obtained at the Christmas examination is generally more honourable than any other, because it shows that the person who receives it is the first in literary merit. He had Burke as a contemporary. Goldsmith had the reputation of being able to turn an ode of Horace into English better than any of them. He afterwards studied physic at Edinburgh and upon the Continent, pursuing his travels on foot, partly by demanding at universities to enter the lists as a disputant, by which, according to the custom of some of them, he became entitled to a premium of a crown, when, luckily for him, his challenge was not accepted, so that, Boswell suggested to Johnson, he *disputed* his passage through Europe. Returned to England, he was usher in an academy, a corrector of the press, a reviewer, and a writer for a newspaper. He had sagacity enough to cultivate the acquaintance of Dr. Johnson, and his mind was invigorated by conversations with him. John Newbery, too, found that in him he could secure help for publications he was producing, and engaged his services accordingly, to their mutual advantage. Children's lives interested him, and for them and their interests he devoted much earnest work. Some time elapsed before he ventured to let the public know him by name as an author. No man had the art of displaying with more advantage as a writer whatever literary acquisitions he made. " Nihil quod tetigit non ornavit," Dr. Johnson's view of him, is on his epitaph in Westminster Abbey: an opinion no one would despise and all could consider he deserved. His mind resembled a fertile but thin soil. There was a quick but not strong vegetation of whatever chanced to be thrown upon it. No deep root could be struck. The oak did not grow there, but the elegant shrubbery and the fragrant parterre appeared in gay succession. His character was simple, and many were amused at his sallies and mistakes.

At an evening gathering in Fleet Street of the club attended by savants and wits, he found in the chair, before the proceedings commenced, a handsomely dressed man, and, guessing his importance by his appearance, set him down as some notability in the City, and enquiring who he might be, was told he was "the Master of the Rolls." He was a baker. Horace Walpole admired his writings. David Garrick described him as one "for shortness call'd Noll, who wrote like an angel and talked like poor Poll." His share of that hurry of ideas which is sometimes found in his countrymen, joined to his charitable disposition, made him the sport of fancy, and led him into extravagances which were at times serious, at others comical. Sir Joshua Reynolds heard Goldsmith talk warmly of the pleasure of being liked, and observed how hard it would be if literary excellence should preclude a man from that satisfaction, which he perceived it often did, from the envy which attended it. Whilst accompanying two beautiful young ladies (the Misses Horneck) with their mother on a tour in France, he was seriously angry that more attention was paid to them than to him; and at an exhibition of the Fantoccini in London, when those sitting next to him observed with what dexterity a puppet was made to toss a pike, he could not bear that it should have such praise, and exclaimed with some warmth, "Pshaw! I can do it better myself."

Washington Irving tells us a prominent employer of Goldsmith was Mr. John Newbery, who engaged him to contribute occasional essays to a newspaper called "The Public Ledger," which made its first appearance on January 12th, 1760. "His most valuable and characteristic contributions were his 'Chinese Letters,' subsequently modified into 'The Citizens of the World.' These lucubrations attracted general attention. They were reprinted in various periodical publications of the day, and met with great applause. The name of the author, however, was, as yet, but little known."

Goldsmith's connection with Newbery, the publisher, now led him into a variety of temporary jobs, such as "A Life of Beau Nash," the famous master of ceremonies at Bath, &c. Few works, it has been observed by one of his biographers, exhibit a nicer perception or more delicate delineation of life and manners. Wit, humour, and sentiment pervade every page; the vices and follies of the day are touched with the most playful and diverting satire; and English characteristics in endless variety are hit off with the pencil of a master.

Among the various productions thrown off by him for the booksellers was a small work in two volumes entitled "The History of England, in a Series of Letters from a Nobleman to his Son." It was digested from Hume, Rapin, Carte, and Kennett. These authors he would read in the morning, make a few notes, ramble with a friend into the country, return to a temperate dinner and cheerful evening, and would, before going to bed, write off what had arranged itself in his head from the studies of the morning. It was anonymous. Lord Lyttelton seemed pleased to be thought the author, and never disowned the bantling thus laid at his door. It was ascribed to many noble lords, who blushed but did not disclaim it. They got the credit, and Goldsmith chuckled. The reputation of Goldsmith grew slowly. He was known and estimated by a few. His works were more apt to be felt than talked about. About the beginning of 1763 he became acquainted with Boswell, who was at that time young, light, buoyant, pushing, and presumptuous. He mingled in the society of men noted for wit and learning, and was bent on making his way into the literary circles of the metropolis. An intimacy with Dr. Johnson, the great literary luminary of the day, was the crowning object of his ambition. It was generally understood that Goldsmith was the author of "An Enquiry into the present state of Polite Learning in Europe."

Never since the days of Don Quixote and Sancho Panza had there been a more whimsically contrasted pair of associates than Boswell and Johnson. "Who is this Scotch cur at Johnson's heels?" asked some one when Boswell had worked his way. "He is not a cur," replied Goldsmith. "You are too severe; he is only a burr. Tom Davies flung him at Johnson in sport, and he had the faculty of sticking."

John Williams, bookseller, in Fleet Street, on February 14th, 1765, fared badly: the authorities stood him in the pillory in New Palace Yard, Westminster, for republishing "The North Briton," complete in volumes. The populace defeated the intentions of the ignominy by displaying a burlesque exhibition that excited much more attention and sentiments directly opposite. They suspended near the pillory a jackboot, a Scot's bonnet, and an axe. After suffering them to hang for some time, they chopped off the top of the boot and burned it, together with the bonnet, with great triumph. In the meantime a gentleman, putting a guinea in a purse, handed it round to the assembly, and, it is said, collected two hundred guineas for Mr. Williams's benefit! The hackney coach No. 45 carried him to and from the pillory; nor would the anti-ministerial driver accept anything for the use of the carriage. In 1770 Mr. Bingley, the bookseller, was confined in the King's Bench Prison because he would not answer interrogations in the Court of King's Bench by order of the Court. ("The History of London," edition 1773. Baldwin, 47, Paternoster Row.)

The misfortunes of authors have been proverbial; and what a censure does not that fact pronounce upon the ingratitude of society! The other professions enrich, authorship impoverishes.

> "The rich physician, honoured lawyers, ride,
> While the poor scholar foots it by their side."

So the followers of the Muses may have, like Goldsmith, gained fame and an early grave. Oliver Goldsmith, in his forty-sixth year, died a broken-hearted man. Twice he thought of suicide, but was restrained by his belief in Christianity, and lived to immortalise his name. His grave is on the north side of the Temple Church in London. Can we guess the felicity of men of genius in a garret, exercising their faculties for the good of their fellow-creatures or for the glory of God? He did a good work; taught mankind a great lesson, how Christianity can enable the believer to endure to the end and triumph.

When we know that Sir Walter Scott, the master of all the avenues to the human heart, has said, "We read 'The Vicar of Wakefield' in youth and old age, we return to it again and again, and bless the memory of an author who contrives so well to reconcile us to human nature," we are glad Dr. Johnson thought well of it, and showed it to Newbery, the publisher, who sent him down Ludgate Hill to Goldsmith with a pocket full of guineas. Its value then was not known, nor had Newbery read it. But has it not been read, reprinted, and sold by the thousand since? The testimony of the people of all countries confess their delight as they enjoy their favourite volume, and acknowledge with one consent that the discourses of "The Vicar of Wakefield" have reached and consoled their hearts. After completing it, can we compass Goldsmith's feelings as he laid down his pen?

Schlegel, the German critic and scholar, gave it as his opinion that the gem of European works of fiction was "The Vicar of Wakefield." Rogers feelingly observed to Mr. Forster, "that of all the books which through the fitful changes of three generations he had seen rise and fall, the charms of 'The Vicar of Wakefield' had alone continued as at first, and that, could he revisit the world after an interval of many more generations, he should as surely look to find it undiminished."

Even a poet must live! Amongst the most remunerative of Goldsmith's prose publications were his abridgements of English, Roman, and Grecian history, and his "Animated Nature." Lord Macaulay pronounced him a master, perhaps unequalled, in the arts of selection and condensation, adding, "this has hitherto fallen to the lot of very dull men, and they have embarrassed what they undertook to simplify."

Before "The Deserted Village" saw the light, the bookseller gave Goldsmith an advance note for one hundred guineas. Going home, however, Goldsmith told this to a friend, who, judging poetry by quantity rather than quality, called it too great a sum for so small a poem! Goldsmith replied, "I think so too! It is much more than he can afford or the piece is worth. I have not felt comfortable since I took it." He actually gave back the advance note, and asked to be rewarded according to the measure of success of the work. Goldsmith told his brother Charles, when surprised he was no better off, "All in good time, my dear boy; I shall be richer by-and-by. Addison, let me tell you, wrote his poem 'The Campaign' in a garret in the Haymarket, three stories high, and you see I am not come to that yet, for I have only got to the second story."

As a rule, literature, no doubt, is the worst paid of professions. We know what Milton received for "Paradise Lost"; how Goldsmith said, truly enough, that poetry had found him poor, and kept him so; how Otway and Chatterton starved upon it; how Southey gained £3 for an epic; how Wordsworth said his receipts for verse would not pay for his shoe-leather ; and there are living writers whose works, while claiming men of culture, put nothing into their purses.

However this present compilation shall be received, the author's design cannot be disappointed. His appeal to the reader's judgment will show that he does not found his hopes of approbation upon their ignorance, and that he fears their censure least whose knowledge is the most extensive.

REPRINTED
SONS LT
DERBY.
LONDON